THE FINE ART OF
JAPANESE
COOKING

HIDEO DEKURA

BayBooks

An imprint of HarperCollins*Publishers*

NOTE: We developed the recipes in this book in Australia where the tablespoon measure is 20 ml. In many other countries the tablespoon is 15 ml. For most recipes this difference will not be noticeable.

USING CUPS AND SPOONS
All cup and spoon measurements are level

METRIC CUP
¼ cup	60 ml	2 fluid ounces
⅓ cup	80 ml	2½ fluid ounces
½ cup	125 ml	4 fluid ounces
1 cup	250 ml	8 fluid ounces

METRIC SPOONS
¼ teaspoon	1.25 ml
½ teaspoon	2.5 ml
1 teaspoon	5 ml
1 tablespoon	20 ml

A Bay Books Publication

Bay Books, an imprint of
HarperCollins*Publishers*
25 Ryde Road, Pymble, Sydney, NSW 2073, Australia
31 View Road, Glenfield, Auckland 10, New Zealand

First published in Australia in 1984
This edition 1993

National Library of Australia
Cataloguing-in-Publication data:

Dekura, Hideo.
  The fine art of Japanese cooking.

  Includes index.
  ISBN 186378 079 3.

  1. Cookery Japanese. I. Title. (Series: Bay Books cooking collection).
641.5952

Photography by Ashley Barber
Cover styling by William Petley

Hideo Dekura is Director of Japanese Functions of Sydney,
93 Pacific Highway, North Sydney, NSW 2060
Tel: 955 8536 Fax: 954 4706

Printed in Singapore

9 8 7 6 5 4 3 2 1
96 95 94 93

CONTENTS

DISCOVER THE FINE ART OF
JAPANESE COOKING

The preparation, serving and eating of Japanese food is much more than simply a means of satisfying hunger. It is an integral part of the fabric of Japanese culture, interwoven with aesthetics, tradition, religion and history.

The two cardinal rules of Japanese cooking are that food must be very fresh and that it must look beautiful when served. Japanese cuisine is uniquely refined, fastidious and subtle. Whereas Western cooking tends to blend flavours, the Japanese prefer to retain the individual taste and appearance of each element in a dish. Each is relished separately for its own unique qualities. Food is served in small, meticulously prepared portions. Fish plays a very important role, and the Japanese have devised an amazing number of ways to prepare it.

The essence of Japanese cooking is its closeness to nature. Making the most of fresh, natural, seasonal foods with the greatest possible culinary artistry is its keynote. When the strawberries arrive in February for example, they appear everywhere — in the best, most elegant restaurants and on the dinner tables of the humblest households. There are dozens of such foods — fruit, vegetables, fish, and eggs of various birds such as quail — which are forever linked, for the Japanese, with a particular season. Every food has its season and every season its food. The Western preoccupation with exotic and out of season foods is regarded as quite peculiar.

To the uninitiated palate the tastes and textures of Japanese food may seem strange and even distasteful at first. Rest assured that many a reluctant sampler has become in time a devotee. One-pot meals such as sukiyaki and shabu shabu are probably the most easily accessible and satisfying to the westerner. Teriyaki (literally 'shining grill') dishes are also popular. But the subtler delights of a delectably fresh sashimi or a decorative tray of delicate sushi once experienced are never to be forgotten.

Traditional Japanese cooking, some feel,

is in danger of a severe decline because of modern tastes for convenience foods. Western-style restaurants and fast food chains flourish all over Japan. Ironically, Japanese food is fast gaining popularity in the West where Zen austerity has had a marked influence on cooking in recent years — the popularity of *nouvelle cuisine* and *cuisine minceur* bears witness to this. As well, general taste now tends more towards lighter, simpler meals and away from the richer dishes of classical cooking. People are more health conscious about their diets. They do not want to eat as much as in the past and are not as dependent on fats, dairy products and sugar.

To better understand the distinctive approach of the Japanese to food and eating, it helps to know something of their history and culture.

HISTORY

The worship of nature by the ancient Japanese laid the foundation for the national cuisine. This, and the fact that Japan has never produced crop surpluses because of its mountainous terrain, gave rise to two important elements in Japanese cooking — freshness and frugality. Contact with other peoples added other elements which the Japanese modified and made truly their own.

From the sixth through to the eighth centuries Japan had considerable contact with China, a more complex and sophisticated culture. The Chinese cultural influence was felt profoundly in all aspects of life including cuisine. Buddhism, with its deep respect for all forms of life and its prohibition of meat eating, was particularly influential. Tea and soybeans were both imported from China during this period.

Free contact with China came to an end in the middle of the ninth century with the collapse of the T'ang dynasty. Then followed 400 years known as the Heian age, named after Japan's ancient capital of Heian-kyo (Kyoto). This was a golden age for Japanese culture when art and social life were perfected and refined to an amazing degree. An extremely elaborate code of etiquette developed, governing just about every aspect of life from politics to lovemaking. Although food remained simple and natural, various complicated and decorative ways of presenting it were developed.

After the golden age came several centuries of war and civil strife and the rise to power of the samurai warriors. Savage and warlike though they undoubtedly were, the samurai did however favour ceremonial and elegant table etiquette. The fifteenth century saw the perfection of the Buddhist-inspired tea ceremony, the epitome of frugal refinement.

Toward the middle of the sixteenth century came the first contact with the Western world via some adventurous Portuguese traders. Quite quickly, a flourishing trade relationship was established with Portugal. The Japanese regarded the foreigners as primitive barbarians, albeit shrewd and valuable trading partners. The Jesuit missionaries, led by St Francis Xavier, who followed the merchants, showed more sympathy towards Japanese civilisation. Tempura, that most refined and light of deep-fried dishes, was actually adapted from traditional Portuguese deep-fried food. Of course the Japanese characteristically refined the concept much further.

It was not until after the 1850s that Japan became very open to the influences of Western industrialisation. The Japanese people found much to admire in dynamic capitalist civilisation and took to Western ways with great enthusiasm and amazing success. They made particularly rapid progress in the field of science and technology and by the early twentieth century Japan was well on its way to becoming the industrial giant it is today. At the same time they borrowed Western-style food and cooking and began to abandon the Buddhist vegetarian diet. Nowadays American fast-food chains thrive throughout urban Japan although there is still great respect for the traditional food. The practice of that most Japanese of customs, the tea ceremony, still enjoys enormous popularity and its intricate rules are carefully passed on from generation to generation.

THE TEA CEREMONY

Tea is Japan's national drink and is taken with most meals and at practically any time of the day or night. But a uniquely complex set of rituals and customs known as the tea ceremony has come to be associated with drinking matcha, a special kind of powdered green tea. The tea ceremony is, however, much more than a formal social gathering — it has great aesthetic and spiritual significance which can be said to embody the very essence of the Japanese approach to life.

The historical roots of the tea ceremony reach back to the thirteenth century when Zen Buddhist monks used to drink tea ceremonially to aid them in their devotions. The rituals were elaborated and refined to an art form by the tea masters of the Imperial court of the fifteenth and sixteenth centuries. The many complicated rules laid down by the tea masters governed every aspect of the ceremony from the number of guests to the positioning of vessels and the size and proportions of the tea room. These rules are still observed today.

The vessels are arranged in a harmonious and artistic pattern. They are often objects of great beauty and antiquity in themselves. The host or hostess ritually cleans the teaspoon, tea caddy and the tea bowl with a silk cloth called the 'fukusa'. The tea bowl is then washed with hot water from the traditional iron kettle which simmers over a charcoal fire. With great care and solemnity the green powdered tea is measured into the bowl with a special long bamboo teaspoon. Only the freshest, purest water is used to make the tea and it must be exactly the right temperature — very hot but not boiling or bubbling excessively. Finally the tea in the bowl is whisked, with a 'chasen' or hand-made bamboo whisk, into a jade-coloured froth. The technique required to whip the tea just enough and with a vigorous yet graceful motion can take years to learn. The tea is drunk with formal, graceful movements and every nuance of flavour and aroma savoured fully. A simple tea ceremony takes about forty minutes but if the traditional elegant meal or 'kaiseki' is served it can last for hours.

It is sometimes hard for westerners to understand the fastidious attention to detail so characteristic of the tea ceremony. Our practical, materialistic way of life leaves little room for such leisurely stateliness. For the Japanese however it is a valuable part of their social, cultural and spiritual heritage. Its formality and understated elegance can both refresh the senses and soothe the spirit.

Chicken Pot

JAPANESE
COOKING CLASS

FILLETING SNAPPER

1 *Thoroughly scale fish.*

2 *Holding the fish firmly on the board with your left hand cut into the back below the head with the point of the knife and continue to cut downwards, working as close as possible to the skeleton.*

3 *Repeat this process along the belly and gently lift off the whole fillet.*

4 *Hold the tail in your left hand and cut upwards towards the head, keeping knife just below the skeleton.*

VEGETABLE CUTTING

CARROT

1 *Peel the carrots.*

2 *Cut each carrot in half vertically and then into thin slices.*

3 *Cut each piece lengthwise into even-sized sticks.*

4 *Cut sticks into tiny dice.*

DAIKON

1 *Wash and peel daikon.*
2 *Cut in half lengthwise and slice into half rounds or –*
3 *grate into needle shreds.*

ONION

1 *Peel onion and cut in half lengthwise.*
2 *Slice finely but do not cut through completely.*
3 *Chop into fine dice.*

CABBAGE

1 *Peel off coarse outer leaves.*
2 *Slice in half lengthwise.*
3 *Chop into fairly large pieces.*

TURNIP

1 *Peel and trim turnip.*
2 *Slice into very thin rounds with a sharp vegetable knife.*
3 *Cut rounds into 4 pieces.*

 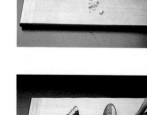

SPRING ONION

1 *Trim spring onions and peel away coarse outer leaves.*
2 *Slice very thinly into diagonal pieces or –*
3 *chop into fine rounds.*

CUCUMBER

1 *Peel one thin slice of peel from each side of cucumber with a vegetable peeler.*
2 *Halve cucumber and scoop out seeds.*
3 *Slice very thinly.*

1 *Carrot, zucchini (courgette), daikon & spray of pine needles, mushroom.*

2 *Pumpkin and cucumber skin.*

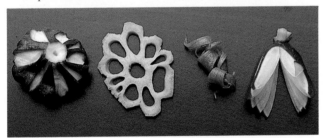

3 *Baby squash, lotus root, spring onion, red radish.*

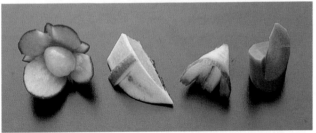

4 *Red radish with ginkgo nut, lemon, cucumber, carrot.*

5 *Cucumber, shredded daikon, daikon leaves, turnip.*

6 *Carrot, cucumber, leek, carrot.*

PRESENTATION GARNISHES

Western visitors to Japanese restaurants are often entranced by the chef's deft and delicate wielding of the vegetable knife — done in full view of diners — to produce decoratively cut and shaped vegetables for presentation garnishes. Quaint and beautiful flowers, leaves, animals and geometric or lace-like patterns adorn platters of sushi and sashimi or clear bowls of soup or dipping sauce.

Although it can take years to master traditional cutting techniques, some garnishes are quite simple to make and it is rewarding to try a few of them for yourself. They make a spectacular presentation and add an aesthetic dimension to cooking not much emphasised in Western cuisine.

The method of cutting and shape vary with the vegetables you have to work with and are designed to make the most of flavour as well as colour and texture. Cylindrical vegetables such as carrot and daikon lend themselves to thin circular or half-moon sections, lotus root to complex lacy patterns and cucumber peel to ribbon-like garnishes. The firm texture of carrot and daikon make them very versatile for garnishes.

7 *Lemon, carrot, cucumber and lemon peel, cucumber, carrot.*

8 *Camellia leaves and green ginger, cucumber peel, cucumber, carrot.*

1 Use a sharp knife to cut the stem off the pumpkin and carefully remove all the seeds.

2 With a sharp tool begin carving approximately 5 cm (2 in) from the top of the pumpkin. Carve away the skin so the top of the pumpkin resembles the neck and lip of a vase.

3 Use a black felt-tipped pen to write the message on the flesh of the pumpkin and carve the skin away from that area. The message written on this one is 'Beautiful Japan'.

4 Continue to carve away the skin to make the lettering stand out.

❖ **VEGETABLE SCULPTURE**

This type of vegetable sculpture is called muki-mono. The muki-mono technique can be used with many different vegetables. The vegetables are sometimes carved to resemble Japanese Ike-Bana flower arrangements. A lot of skill and patience is essential to obtain a perfect sculpture. Ice carving is another decorative technique used in Japanese cuisine.

UTENSILS AND IMPLEMENTS

1 Disposable chopsticks.
2 Bamboo cooking chopsticks.
3 Muki-mono knife.
4 Scraper.
5 Mortar and pestle.
6 Skewer for securing eel to chopping board.
7 Strainer (for fried food).
8 Scoop for fruit or vegetables.
9 Fish scaler.
10 Opener for shellfish.
11 Vegetable cleaver.
12 Fish knife.
13 Steel chopsticks (for sashimi arrangement).
14 Vegetable carving/ chiselling knife.
15 Sashimi knife.

❖ A small bamboo mat (sudare) will be useful for sushi dishes.

JAPANESE CHOPSTICKS

Traditionally all Japanese food except soup is eaten with chopsticks and chopsticks are used to cook with as well.

Japanese chopsticks have pointed ends, unlike the Chinese variety which have blunt ends. They are well suited to Japanese cuisine; extreme care is taken with food presentation and the pointed ends can be used to carefully pick up each piece of food, keeping the arrangement on the platter looking beautiful throughout the meal.

For the Japanese people chopsticks serve as knife, fork and spoon at the table. For everyday meals, short, rounded lacquered chopsticks are used. Formal meals call for special cedarwood chopsticks and on very casual occasions short, flat, wooden, disposable chopsticks with blunt ends may be used. Disposable chopsticks are inexpensive and convenient to use and may be purchased in many oriental stores.

Kitchen chopsticks are two to three times longer than ordinary eating chopsticks. They allow one-handed manipulation of all kinds of food and are useful for all types of Japanese cooking, be it deep frying, pot cooking, sushi making, pickling or the making of desserts.

When setting the table for a Japanese meal, chopsticks are never laid flat on the table. They rest on special chopsticks rests or holders made of porcelain, pottery or bamboo. The chopsticks are placed in front of the guest side by side with both points resting on the holder and facing to the left. Chopsticks facing to the right mean bad luck to the Japanese. Between courses the chopsticks are always placed on the rests. It is considered ill-mannered to place them on the plate or in the bowl.

1 *Hold one chopstick in crook of thumb, resting on inside tip of ring finger.*

2 *Place second chopstick in a similar position, then press it between index and middle fingers with ball of thumb.*

3 *Bend index and middle fingers and slide upper stick down to meet lower one to pick up food.*

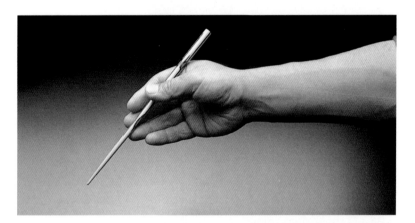

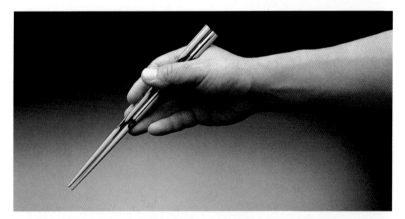

GLOSSARY

AGAR-AGAR (KANTEN) A gelling agent derived from seaweed, this can be purchased as long thin strands, flakes or powder from Asian and health food stores. It is used in a similar manner to gelatine, but has the advantage of setting without refrigeration. Sprinkle with cold water to soften, then cook over medium heat until dissolved (do not stir until dissolved). Strips may also be softened and cut up as a salad ingredient. Keeps indefinitely in a cool, dark cupboard.

AZUKI (ADZUKI) BEANS These are small red beans with a rich sweet flavour, known as the 'king of beans', and are easily available from Asian or health food stores. They are generally sweetened and used for making bean jam or for filling cakes, or may be steamed with sticky rice. If bought dried, the beans need to be soaked overnight in cold water, then cooked until tender (for about 3 hours). A prepared sweet bean paste is also available in cans. The beans will keep for a year in a cool, dark cupboard.

BAMBOO SHOOTS (TAKENOKO) The young shoots of the bamboo plant, used frequently in Asian cooking. Only available fresh at specialist Asian markets, but the canned ones which retain much of the texture and flavour are widely available. Both fresh and opened canned bamboo shoots have a short life and should be refrigerated and used within a few days.

BEAN CURD (TOFU) Tofu is made by coagulating the liquid from soy beans which have been soaked, ground and cooked. It is renowned for being high in protein, and low in cholesterol, fat and calories. It may be purchased fresh or vacuum-packed from Asian and health food stores. It readily absorbs flavour (having only a delicate flavour itself), or it can be used as a neutral contrast to other ingredients. Fresh tofu has a very short life — refrigerate, changing the water daily, and use within 1 week. Inari are bean-curd bags which can be bought cooked or uncooked.

BONITO (KATSUO-BUSHI) A dried fish of the mackerel family, this is preferably bought pre-flaked as it is hard to cut. It can be obtained from Asian or health food stores in flakes or thin shavings. It is used to make stock (dashi), and the shavings are sprinkled over cooked foods and salads as a garnish. If stored in an airtight container keeps for 1 year.

BRACKEN (WARABI) The tender young fronds of the bracken fern, picked before they have uncurled. Mature open fronds may be poisonous, so do not experiment with unknown ferns. The edible kinds are available dried or vacuum-packed at Japanese stores. Cook briefly, or serve raw in salads. Use vacuum-packed bracken by the use-by date, or immediately after opening. Dried bracken will keep for 6 months in a cool, dark place.

CABBAGE, ASIAN (HAKUSAI) This has pale yellow-green leaves with white ribs, and looks like a cross between lettuce and cabbage. It can be obtained from most well stocked markets. It may be steamed, braised, stir-fried, added to soups, used in salads, or pickled. Store refrigerated for up to 1 week.

CHESTNUTS (KURI) These nuts are available in jars in syrup, dried, canned, or fresh in season. The dried ones should be soaked in cold water overnight before use, and simmered until tender. The fresh should be used as soon as possible, though the dried will keep for 1 year.

CHILLIES, RED — DRIED (TOGARASHI) Chillies are a small, hot variety of the capsicum (pepper) family, and dried ones are readily available. Buy the thin, bright-red ones that are about 4 to 5 cm (2 in) long. Chillies should be handled with caution, and the hands washed thoroughly with soap afterwards. Do not touch any sensitive areas such as the eyes or face, or small children, after handling chillies. Chillies are used to add heat to foods, but also in small amounts to 'awaken the taste buds' and enhance other flavours. Store cool, dry and airtight for up to 1 year.

CHRYSANTHEMUM LEAVES (SHUNGIKU) These are related to the garden chrysanthemums (which are also edible), but are a different variety and have a more pronounced flavour. They are available fresh from Asian produce markets. Do not cook them for too long — they may be stir-fried, steamed, or if young and tender, used raw in salads. Store in the refrigerator for up to 1 week.

CLOUD EAR MUSHROOMS (KIKURAGE) These dried black mushrooms are a delight to use. They are also known as wood fungus, tree fungus or black fungus, and can be purchased from Asian stores. Soak in cold water for 10 minutes — they swell considerably, and form curved petal shapes (similar to an ear, hence one of their names). The base of the petal forms a small stalk which should be cut off and discarded if tough. Cloud ears have a delicate flavour of their own but also absorb other flavourings and add a crunchy texture. Cook briefly only, or use raw in salads. They keep indefinitely in a cool, dark cupboard.

CUCUMBER (KYURI) The Japanese variety of cucumber is smaller and has a thinner skin and smaller seeds than Western varieties. Use Lebanese (telegraph) cucumbers if the Japanese ones are not available. Store in the refrigerator as for ordinary ones.

DAIKON A large pale skinned radish which has a more delicate flavour than the common red radish. It can be bought at most well-stocked vegetable markets or at Asian markets. Peel thinly and slice or grate as required, for use either raw or cooked. Daikon may also be pickled. Finely grated daikon for use as a relish or flavouring should be drained to rid it of excess moisture. Daikon is an aid to digestion and will also assist tenderisation of meat in braised dishes. Store in the refrigerator for up to 1 week.

DASHI A classic Japanese seasoning made normally from dried kelp (*see* Stocks and Soups, p. 66). It is also available as an 'instant' powder.

EGGS, QUAIL (AZURA NO TAMAGO) Although similar in flavour to chicken eggs, these dainty little eggs are preferred because of their convenient size. They can be bought cooked, in cans or jars, but are also available fresh in Asian food stores and in good poultry shops. Store in the refrigerator for up to 2 weeks.

ENOKITAKE MUSHROOMS (ENOKITAKE) These are tiny golden-yellow capped mushrooms with a long stalk and a very delicate flavour. They are available fresh from specialist vegetable markets or canned from Asian stores (the

canned ones lose texture and flavour). Fresh ones should be rinsed and the lower 2 cm (1 in) of the stalks trimmed off. They may be eaten raw in salads, or used as a garnish, or cooked in soups and other savoury dishes. Do not overcook, as they will soften and lose their crisp texture and may become bitter. Refrigerate and use within 1 to 2 days.

FISH PASTE (KAMABOKO) A steamed, puréed fish product which can be bought at Asian stores. Since it is pre-cooked, it can be sliced and served cold with dipping sauces or reheated in soups and savoury dishes. Refrigerate and use as soon as possible (within 1 week).

GINGER (SHOGA OR SYOU-GA) Ginger is the pungent rhizome (underground stem) of the ginger plant and is one of the most popular ingredients in Asian cooking. It is readily available, but avoid old withered pieces and buy plump, firm-skinned ones. If fresh and young, the skin can be scraped off with a teaspoon; otherwise peel thinly. Slice, chop or grate as required. Store in a dry, airy basket, or peeled and sliced in dry sherry in the refrigerator. It can also be frozen, but prepare beforehand as the ginger will be very soft and watery when defrosted. Japanese pickled ginger (red or pink) can be purchased from Asian stores.

GINKGO NUTS (GINNAN) The kernels of the fruit of the maidenhair tree, these are ivory coloured with a delicate flavour. Available in cans from Asian stores and fresh from Japanese stores. Fresh ones must be shelled and blanched before use (pour boiling water over them, stand for 5 minutes, then remove the skins). They are often used as a garnish in soups, fried or poached dishes. Refrigerate and use as soon as possible.

GINSENG A plant found in China, Korea, Nepal, Canada and eastern USA. It has a branching root which is thought to resemble a man, and is credited with having restorative powers. Its main use is medicinal though it may be used in cooking. Ginseng, as infusions or tea, is a popular tonic for many ailments. Can be purchased from Asian or health food stores.

GLUTINOUS RICE FLOUR (MOCHIKO) Flour made from glutinous rice, this has a sweet flavour and is used mainly for desserts. Store in a cool, dry cupboard for up to 1 year.

GOURD SHAVINGS, DRIED (KAMPYO) Flexible, beige coloured ribbons of dried gourd, available from Asian and health food stores. They should be softened in warm water before use (about 20 minutes). Their main use is as an edible 'string' for tying parcels and bundles of food, but they may also be used as a garnish. Kampyo keeps indefinitely in a cool, dark cupboard.

KATA-KURIKO A Japanese starch made from potato, used as a thickener. Arrowroot may be substituted in equal amounts, or use twice as much cornflour.

KELP (KONBU) A dried seaweed, also known as sea-tangle. Readily available from Asian and health food stores. It is used as a flavouring for soups and stocks, and as a wrapping for foods; cooked as a vegetable; pickled; or used in salads. It should be wiped with a damp cloth before use, and the surface may be lightly scored to extract more flavour. Keeps for about 6 months in a cool dry cupboard.

KINOME Young leaves from the same tree that produces the fragrant Szechuan peppercorns. Seasonally available fresh from Japanese markets. If using whole sprigs as a garnish, bruise lightly with the heel

1. Azuki beans
2. Dried cloud ear mushrooms
3. Dried gourd shavings
4. Black and white sesame seeds and rice
5. Wheat noodles
6. Dried shiitake mushrooms
7. Candied chestnuts
8. Rice noodles
9. Ponzu sauce
10. Mirin wine
11. Rice vinegar
12. Konyaku paste
13. Wasabi paste
14. Wasabi powder

MIRIN WINE A sweet rice wine, extensively used as a flavouring in Japanese cooking and readily available from Asian stores. It contains alcohol which generally boils off in the cooking, or it may be boiled off beforehand. As well as flavouring, it is often used as a glaze to enhance the appearance of cooked foods. Keeps for several months in a cool, dark cupboard or can be refrigerated for longer life.

MISO A fermented soybean paste. There are several varieties, based on whether grains (rice or barley) are combined with the soy beans, and how long they are fermented. The two most popular are white miso made with young rice, which is lighter and more delicate, and red miso which is fermented for longer and has a more robust flavour. Miso can be purchased from Asian and health food shops. It is used for flavouring soups, marinades, sauces and glazes, and is a valuable source of the B group vitamins in vegetarian diets. Store in the refrigerator for 1 year.

MOCHI This is cooked glutinous rice which has been pounded to a paste, and then cut or moulded into shape. It is available ready prepared from Asian stores but may easily be made at home. Generally grilled with a glaze of mirin or saké, the rice cakes will swell in the cooking

of the hand to release more flavour. They may also be chopped or ground to use in salad dressings. They have a lovely, crisp, fresh, slightly minty flavour. Refrigerate, and use within a few days of purchase.

KUZU A Japanese starch made from the kuzu plant. Can be purchased from Asian or health food stores, but it is expensive. Arrowroot may be substituted, but use twice as much to get an equivalent thickness. Keeps indefinitely.

LOTUS ROOT (RENKON) Used more for eye-appeal than for flavour, this root vegetable has hollow tubes along its length which give a lacy pattern when the root is sliced across. May be available fresh from Asian vegetable markets, or vacuum-packed, dried or canned,

from Asian food stores. The fresh root needs to be peeled before use, and all forms should be cooked in water with vinegar or lemon juice added to stop discolouration. The dried ones should be soaked in warm water with lemon juice for 1 hour before use. Dried lotus root keeps indefinitely, while the fresh root should be refrigerated and used within 10 days.

MATSUTAKE MUSHROOMS These large brown Japanese mushrooms grow wild on red pine trees (they are also called 'pine mushrooms'). They are very expensive and can be obtained fresh for only a very brief season in Japanese markets. Canned ones are available but do not have a comparable flavour. Use fresh mushrooms as soon as possible after purchase.

and develop a tasty crust. Mochi will keep refrigerated for a few days or, if frozen, for up to 5 months.

MUSTARD (KARASHI) Ground yellow mustard seeds in a fine powder form — this is very pungent. Make sure you buy only ground mustard seeds, as some prepared powders contain other ingredients. Mix to a paste with an equal quantity of warm water, cover and leave for 5 minutes for the flavour to develop. Do not prepare too far in advance as the heat will dissipate. Mustard is used as a condiment and in sauces and salad dressings. Mustard powder will keep for 1 year in a cool dark cupboard.

NAMEKO MUSHROOMS These are available from Asian stores and are usually labelled 'Straw Mushrooms'. They are small unopened mushrooms with the cap completely enclosing the stalk, and have a very appealing flavour, although the slippery texture may be less appealing to Western palates. Unused portions of opened cans should be refrigerated in a jar and used within a few days.

NORI SEAWEED (NORI) Thin sheets of dried seaweed, either deep purple (untoasted) or dark green (toasted). These are available from most Asian and health food shops. The purple sheets should be held with tongs over a gas flame or a hotplate for a few seconds until they turn green. (The pre-toasted ones will also benefit from a light toasting before use.) Nori is used for wrapping filled rolls of sushi rice, and also as a seasoning and a garnish. Store airtight in a cool, dark place for up to 6 months.

OIL (ABURA) For Asian cooking, use only light flavoured vegetable oils (olive oil is definitely too strong and too alien a flavour to use). Peanut oil is preferable for frying as it does not oxidise as readily as other oils when heated. The oriental sesame oil, made from toasted sesame seeds, is used in small amounts as a flavouring, not a cooking medium. Most oils will keep up to 6 months or longer if stored in a cool, dark cupboard.

PEARS, ASIAN (NASHI) Asian pears have a lovely crisp texture, even when ripe, and are not as sweet as European varieties. They have a similar shape to an apple and are a brown to golden colour. They are available fresh from many fruit markets, or canned from Asian food stores. Store the same way as Western pears.

RICE BRAN (NUKA) Nuka is the bran (outer husk) of rice. It is available in Asian and specialist Japanese stores. In Japan it is generally used with salt and sometimes other flavourings to pickle vegetables. Store airtight in a cool dark cupboard for 3 months, or refrigerate for longer life.

RICE FLOUR (JOSHINKO) Flour made from short grain rice, this is used in savoury doughs, wrappers and pastries. Store in a cool, dry cupboard for up to 1 year.

SAKÉ A Japanese rice wine which is a very popular beverage and is also used as a seasoning in cooking. It is available from most well-stocked licensed outlets. Saké is traditionally used to counteract fish flavours and excess saltiness, and it contains some amino acids which help to tenderise meat. Most of the alcohol in saké will evaporate in the cooking, although it can be boiled or burnt off before use. Store in a cool, dry place for a year, or refrigerate for longer life.

SANSHO Also known as Szechuan peppercorns, these are small red-brown rough-surfaced seed pods of the prickly ash tree. They can be purchased from Asian stores either whole or pre-ground. The whole ones should be dry-roasted in a small pan over medium heat until fragrant (2 to 3 minutes) and then ground in a blender or a pepper mill. Store airtight in a cool dark cupboard for 6 months.

SESAME SEEDS (GOMA) These are available as white hulled seeds, beige coloured unhulled seeds, or black unhulled seeds. The white are commonly available, and the beige and black can be obtained from Asian and health food stores. They all have a delightful, nutty flavour, which is enhanced by dry-roasting in a small pan over medium heat for 3 to 4 minutes until fragrant. They can be used whole as a garnish, or ground to flavour sauces, marinades, salads and sweets. The black ones provide stunning colour contrast when used as a garnish on pale coloured foods. Sesame seeds have a high oil content, so store them in the refrigerator to stop them turning bitter and rancid.

SEVEN SPICE MIXTURE (SHICHIMI TOGARASHI) A finely ground mixture including mustard, sesame and poppy seeds, peppercorns, nori seaweed and tangerine peel. It is available in small jars in Asian stores and is used to season many Japanese dishes. Store airtight in a cool dry place for 3 months, or refrigerate for longer life.

SHIITAKE MUSHROOMS These are grown on the soft bark of water-soaked logs and have brown caps with tan coloured gills (under-surface). They are available from Asian and some health food stores. They can be soaked for 30 minutes in hot water to soften them, but retain more flavour if soaked in cool water for 5 to 6 hours. The stems are quite tough and are usually discarded or used to flavour stocks and sauces. Store airtight in a cool dry place for 1 year.

SOBA NOODLES Noodles made from buckwheat flour, grey in colour, and usually very thin. They can be purchased in Asian and some health food stores. Cook briefly only, and serve hot in soup or broth, or serve chilled with a dipping sauce. Keep indefinitely in a cool, dark cupboard.

SOMEN NOODLES Noodles made from wheat flour, these are thin to very thin, and often packed with individual servings tied in a ribbon. They are available fresh from Japanese stores and dried from Asian and health food stores. Keep indefinitely in a cool, dark place.

SOY BEAN FLOUR (KINAKO) A high protein flour with a pronounced flavour. It is generally used in making sweetmeats. It has a very short life, so keep refrigerated and use within a few weeks.

SOY BEANS (DAIZU AND EDAMAME) Fresh ones are cooked as a vegetable, or cooled and served in salads. they are available from Asian vegetable markets. The dried beans require long cooking — they can be bought at Asian or health food stores. Soy beans are processed to make bean curd, soy sauce and miso, and may be sprouted. The fresh beans should be used immediately, while the dried ones keep indefinitely.

SOY SAUCE (SHOYU) A thin, dark, salty liquid, prepared from soy beans, wheat and salt (wheat-free and salt-reduced varieties are produced). Readily available, though the better brands, and a greater variety are stocked only at Asian and some health food stores. The light soy sauce is thinner and paler in colour and should be used for pale coloured meats or vegetables, or where a more delicate soy flavour is required. Keeps for 6 months or longer if refrigerated.

SPINACH (HOURENSO) If Japanese spinach is not available, substitute young English spinach rather than silver-beet.

TAMARI A thick soy sauce with a mellow flavour. Can be purchased from health food and Asian stores. This is fermented for a shorter time than other soy sauces, and does not keep as well. Store in the refrigerator after opening.

UDON NOODLES Thick Japanese noodles made from wheat flour. They vary in thickness and in width but are usually flat and oblong in cross section. They can be bought fresh or dried from Asian and health food stores. They will keep indefinitely.

UMEBOSHI A sour, salty pickled plum which is coloured pink by the addition of red shiso leaves. Readily available from Asian or health food stores, either whole or in a paste. These are considered a digestive, and may be eaten whole as a pickle. Alternatively, they may be pitted and ground to add flavour to vegetable dishes or sauces and dressings. They will keep indefinitely in the refrigerator.

VINEGAR (SU) Japanese rice vinegar is milder than most Western vinegars (usually 4 per cent acidity), and may be bought from Asian and health food stores. Keeps indefinitely.

WAKAME SEAWEED (WAKAME) A dried seaweed sold in Asian and health food stores. The strands should be soaked in warm water for 5 minutes if they are to be cooked (which is a short process of only 1 to 2 minutes), or for up to 20 minutes (until tender) if to be used in salads. The strands will turn green after soaking. Stored airtight in a cool dry place, they will keep indefinitely.

WASABI HORSERADISH The root of a Japanese plant, often compared to the Western horseradish. It is similarly pungent, but has a different flavour, and the two are not interchangeable. Wasabi is available from Asian and health food stores in the powdered form, or as a prepared paste in a tube. The powder should be mixed with an equal quantity of cold water, then allowed to stand, covered, for 5 minutes for the flavour to develop. (It will lose heat with prolonged standing, so prepare freshly each time.) The powder keeps indefinitely in a cool, dry place, and the tubes of paste should be refrigerated after opening.

WHEAT GLUTEN (FU) A high protein product made from gluten flour, this can be purchased in a dried form from Asian stores. Soak in warm water to soften and swell, then press out the excess water and add to noodle dishes, soups, and braised dishes. Stored airtight in a cool dry place, it keeps indefinitely.

YAMA-GOBOU A thin root vegetable more often known as burdock root, this can be bought at specialist Asian markets. It is usually cooked unpeeled, as much of the flavour is just below the skin. It discolours on exposure to air, so should be put into water with vinegar or lemon juice added to prevent oxidation. Use as soon as possible, as it has a short life.

YUZU CITRON Citron is an oriental fruit of the citrus family. It is yellow, larger than lemons and with a less acid flavour and a thicker rind. The grated rind and the juice are used to flavour soups, sauces and other dishes. You can substitute lemon or lime juice or rind, although the flavour will be different.

SUSHI

Sushi is extremely popular both with westerners and with the Japanese people themselves. Indeed there are more sushi restaurants in Japan than any other kind. It is true for many people that once tasted sushi quickly become a passion. The natural taste of fresh raw fish and shellfish is a perfect complement to the delicately vinegared rice on which it is served.

There are a number of varieties of sushi using different ingredients and prepared in various ways. But all varieties include the vinegared sushi rice, all are served in bite-sized pieces and all are presented with great care and artistry.

Combination Sushi Platter

STEP-BY-STEP TECHNIQUES

❖ **SUSHI RICE**

There are two main types of rice grown throughout the world — the Japanese variety (Japonica) and the Indian variety (Indica). Japanese-style rice has short, round grains and is sticky when cooked. Indian-style rice has long, narrow grains that, even when cooked, remain loose and separate. Long grain rice is good sauced with oriental foods but does not lend itself to sushi because of its dryness.

Rice that is still firm and resilient when steamed is preferred for nigiri-zushi and rolled sushi. A softer steamed rice is better for moulded sushi.

1 Ingredients: rice, rice vinegar, mirin, sugar, salt.

2 Pour vinegar mixture into rice in hangiri.

3 Run spoon or spatula through rice to separate grains.

4 Prepared sushi rice.

TO PREPARE SUSHI RICE

2½ cups (15 oz/460 g) short-grain rice
3 cups (24 fl oz/750 ml) water

VINEGAR MIXTURE
5 tablespoons rice vinegar
1 tablespoon mirin
3 tablespoons sugar
2 teaspoons salt

1 Wash rice under tap until water runs clear. Drain in a fine strainer for 1 hour. Put the rice in a rice cooker or pot with a tight-fitting lid and add the water. Bring to the boil, reduce heat and boil for a further 5 minutes. Lower heat and steam for 12 to 15 minutes. Take off heat. Remove lid and cover pot with a teatowel. Replace lid and let stand for 15 minutes.

2 TO PREPARE VINEGAR MIXTURE: While rice is cooking, combine vinegar mixture ingredients in a bowl and heat gently till sugar has dissolved, stirring constantly. Remove from heat and cool.

3 Spread rice evenly over the base of a hangiri or other non-metallic tub with a large wooden spoon. Run spatula through the rice to separate the grains, slowly adding vinegar mixture at the same time. The rice should not be too moist.

4 Ask someone to fan the rice with a fan (uchiwa) or a large piece of cardboard until the rice reaches room temperature.

5 Keep rice in the tub covered with a clean cloth until ready for use. Sushi rice lasts only one day and should not be served again.

TO PREPARE SUSHI PRAWNS

Prawns (shrimps) to be used as sushi topping must be well coloured and shaped and carefully opened out to encase the fine finger of sushi rice underneath. Simply prepare and chill until required.

1 Before poaching, slide a bamboo skewer under the shell just above the legs of each prawn to prevent it curling. The skewer should not touch the flesh.

2 Poach lightly in salted water, until the flesh changes colour. Remove from water, drain and slide skewer from the prawn.

3 Remove the head and shell leaving the tail attached. Trim the small pieces of shell from above the tail. This requires patience and a very sharp knife.

4 Carefully make an incision along the underside of the prawn.

5 Deepen the incision so that the prawn can be opened and flattened. Do not cut all the way through as the prawn will fall apart.

6 Devein the prawn.

7 Lightly press the prawn flat to prepare it for use as a topping.

TUNA ROLL (TEKKA-MAKI)

5 half-sheets dried seaweed

3 cups (15 oz/470 g) sushi rice

1 tablespoon wasabi

thinly sliced fresh tuna

1 Spread a layer of rice over one piece of seaweed. Spread a small amount of wasabi evenly over the rice and place some thinly sliced tuna on top.

2 Gently but firmly roll the seaweed up to form a long, thin cylinder. Using a sharp knife cut along the cylinder to form rounds approximately 2½ cm (1 in) wide. Arrange on a dish and serve.

SERVES 4

CALIFORNIAN ROLL (TEMAKI-ZUSHI)

As its name implies, this is a very new, modern type of Japanese maki-zushi. The ingredients and method are the same as for traditional maki-zushi except that the hands are used for rolling instead of a bamboo mat. Maki-zushi consists of vinegared rice, vegetables and fish tightly rolled in seaweed with the aid of a bamboo mat. Temaki-zushi however should not be tightly rolled. By using the hands the filling remains loose.
Temaki-zushi is currently enjoying a worldwide vogue. It is quite simple to prepare and is a good dish to serve when entertaining.

2 sheets dried seaweed, cut in half

1 avocado, peeled and cut into small pieces

1 small cucumber, peeled, seeded and thinly sliced

1 cup (5 oz/155 g) sushi rice

1 teaspoon toasted sesame seeds

1 tin salmon caviar

1 Spread a piece of seaweed with ¼ cup (2 oz/60 g) rice. Sprinkle ¼ teaspoon toasted sesame seeds over the rice. Place 2 slices of cucumber over the sesame seeds. Divide the caviar into 4 and spread 1 portion over the cucumber. Finally place some of the avocado over the caviar and using both hands roll up loosely.

2 Repeat method until all ingredients are used. Each temaki-zushi should be about 10 cm (4 in) long.

SERVES 4

❖ **HOW TO EAT SUSHI**

The preferred ways to eat sushi are with chopsticks or with the fingers. To eat with the fingers: With thumb, index and middle fingers simply pick up a piece of nigiri-zushi and turn it over. Dip only the topping (not the rice) in soy sauce. Slide the sushi into your mouth with the topping facing downwards so it comes into immediate contact with the taste buds. Only a small amount of soy sauce should accompany sushi, to complement not camouflage its delicate flavour.

ROLLED OMELETTE (KOBANA-MAKI)

2 thin Japanese omelettes (see p. 74)

2 pieces dried seaweed

1 cup (5 oz/155 g) sushi rice

½ cucumber, peeled and thinly sliced in long strips

1 x 7½ cm (3 in) piece pickled horseradish, thinly sliced in long strips

⅛ teaspoon wasabi

1 Make omelettes and allow to cool.

2 Place 1 sheet of dried seaweed onto a bamboo mat (sudare). Take 1 omelette and lay over the seaweed. Divide the sushi rice into 2 portions and spread 1 portion over the omelette. Gently press down onto the rice with hands to flatten slightly.

3 Divide cucumber and horseradish into 2 portions. Place half the strips of cucumber and horseradish over the rice. Spread a tiny amount of wasabi over the vegetables.

4 Using both hands and pressing firmly, bring the bamboo mat up from underneath and roll to form a long cylinder. Remove the mat and using a sharp knife, cut the roll into 5 cm (2 in) lengths.

5 Follow the same procedure for the remaining ingredients. Arrange on a plate and serve.

SERVES 4

UNCLAD SEAWEED ROLL (HADAKA-MAKI)

1 cup (5 oz/155 g) sushi rice

2 pieces dried seaweed

⅛ teaspoon wasabi

2 thin slices cucumber

1 square omelette

1 Cut a sheet of plastic wrap and use it to cover a chopping board. Place sushi rice on the plastic wrap and flatten, pressing firmly. Layer both sheets of seaweed over the rice.

Spread wasabi over the seaweed. Place the 2 slices of cucumber across the length of the seaweed. Place the omelette on top as the final layer.

2 Gently lift the plastic wrap from the board and roll the ingredients up firmly using the hands. Use a bamboo mat outside the plastic as an aid to shaping the hadaka-maki into a rectangle.

3 Carefully remove the mat and plastic from the roll and using a sharp knife cut into 2½ cm (1 in) lengths. Arrange on a dish and serve.

SERVES 4

BABY SNAPPER (SUZUME-ZUSHI)

Salting prior to marinating fish in vinegar is called shimeru in Japan.

1 baby snapper (about 10 cm [4 in] long)

salt

MARINADE

1 cup (8 fl oz/250 ml) white vinegar

2 tablespoons sugar

pinch salt

½ cup (4 fl oz/125 ml) dashi

¼ cup (2 fl oz/60 ml) mirin wine

1 Clean and scale baby snapper. Remove head, leaving fins and tail intact. Run knife down spine of the fish and open out butterfly style. Remove backbone.

2 Sprinkle snapper with salt and allow to stand 10 minutes.

3 TO PREPARE MARINADE: Combine all marinade ingredients.

4 Wash salt off the fish, and place in the marinade for half an hour.

5 Use for nigiri-zushi (see p. 21).

SERVES 2

STEP-BY-STEP TECHNIQUES

HAND-SHAPED SUSHI (NIGIRI-ZUSHI)

Nigiri-zushi are made of raw fish wrapped around a core of moulded sushi rice. Nigiri means 'squeezed' in Japanese.

1 Using a sharp knife, cut the baby snapper into thin slices. Place a little mustard onto the sliced fish.

2 Hold a slice in the left hand and mould a rice ball smaller than the slice of fish with the right hand.

3 Place the rice ball on the slice of fish in your left hand.

4 Using both hands mould the fish around the rice gently.

5 Flatten slightly and form into a rectangular shape. Using two fingers, make an indentation across the top of the rectangle, flattening it slightly. The sushi should be 5 cm (2 in) long.

1 Cut flesh into long, thick pieces.

2 Using a fish knife slice pieces very thinly on a slight angle.

3 Place rice ball onto a slice of fish.

4 Gently mould fish around rice.

1 Spread a layer of rice over seaweed on bamboo mat.

2 Place cucumber on rice spread with wasabi.

3 Roll up bamboo mat.

4 Cut into 2½ cm (1 in) rounds.

CUCUMBER ROLL (KAPPA-MAKI)

5 half-sheets dried seaweed
3 cups (15 oz/470 g) sushi rice
1 tablespoon wasabi
½ cucumber, thinly sliced

1 Spread a layer of rice over 1 piece of seaweed. Spread a small amount of wasabi evenly over the rice and place some sliced cucumber on top.

2 Using a bamboo mat gently but firmly roll the seaweed up to form a long, thin cylinder. Using a sharp knife cut along the cylinder at regular intervals to form rounds approximately 2½ cm (1 in) wide.

3 Arrange the kappa-maki on a dish to serve.

SERVES 4 TO 6

Morikomi-zushi is a combination of sushi arranged and served in one large container. Nigiri-zushi, maki-zushi and even oshi-zushi are all suitable for presentation in this way. An arrangement of morikomi-zushi looks very attractive and is convenient to eat, making it an ideal party dish.

Rolled Omelette (p. 20) and Unclad Seaweed Roll (p. 20)

SEA EEL TOKYO-STYLE (ANAGO)

1 sea eel about 30 cm (12 in) long

STOCK
1 cup (8 fl oz/250 ml) water
½ cup (4 oz/125 g) sugar
1½ tablespoons mirin wine
½ cup (4 fl oz/125 ml) soy sauce
50 g (1½ oz) rock sugar (candy), optional

1 Clean the eel and remove head and bones but do not discard. Fillet eel from the back and open out butterfly style.

2 TO PREPARE STOCK: In a saucepan combine the water, sugar, mirin wine and soy sauce. Add eel head and bones and heat over a moderate flame to make a stock.

3 When mixture is hot, add filleted eel and cook on low heat for half an hour.

4 Remove fillets and continue to heat anago sauce (containing the head and bones), over medium heat until thick. The rock sugar may be added at this time to enhance flavour. Strain. This sauce is called nitsume and can be used whenever a fish stock is required.

5 The anago fish is formed into rectangles with sushi rice the same way as nigiri-zushi (see p. 21). The nitsume is brushed over the moulded anago prior to serving.

SERVES 4

FANCY FISH (SAIKU-ZUSHI)

½ cup (3 oz/90 g) sushi rice
1 sheet dried seaweed, cut into 5 pieces
skin of ½ a cucumber
1 small cuttlefish
30 g (2 oz) caviar

1 Form sushi rice into 5 balls and flatten with the fingers to a diameter of 4½ cm (2 in). Carefully wrap the seaweed around each ball of sushi rice.

2 Using a sharp knife cut skin of the cucumber into 5 garnishes, one for each ball. Arrange the 5 balls on a serving dish and place a cucumber garnish on each one.

3 Clean and skin the cuttlefish (see p. 28). Cut flesh into small squares and place one square as a garnish on each rice ball.

4 Using a teaspoon, place a small portion of caviar on the top of each cuttlefish square and serve.

SERVES 2

CAMELLIA SUSHI (CAMELLIA-ZUSHI)

When catering for large groups allow one 'camellia' per person.

½ cup (3 oz/90 g) sushi rice
100 g (3 oz) sashimi tuna fish
1 hard-boiled egg yolk
camellia leaves, to garnish

1 Using both hands mould sushi rice into a ball.

2 Cut the tuna into 4 thin slices, sashimi style. Using one slice of fish at a time, press onto the ball of sushi rice and shape to resemble the petals of the camellia flower. Continue to do so until all 4 slices of tuna are used. (The top of the rice ball should be visible and not covered by the fish.)

3 Pass the egg yolk through a strainer to produce fine threads of yolk. Carefully sprinkle the yolk over the centre of your 'flower' to represent the pollen.

4 Arrange camellia leaves or any similar green garnish around the base of the flower and serve.

PRESSED SUSHI/ BATTERA SUSHI/ (OSHI-ZUSHI BATTERA-ZUSHI)

Oshi-zushi is made using a special oshi-zushi container which is simply a square frame with a lid but no base. To make battera-zushi correctly, an oshi-zushi container is essential. It is also essential that slimy mackerel be used.

sufficient sushi rice to fill an oshi-zushi container

1 x 25 cm (10 in) slimy mackerel

1 large piece dried kelp

MARINADE

1 cup (8 fl oz/250 ml) white vinegar

2 tablespoons sugar

pinch salt

½ cup (4 fl oz/125 ml) dashi

¼ cup (2 fl oz/60 ml) mirin wine

1 Prepare slimy mackerel in same manner as baby snapper (see p. 20). Place in bowl with the dried kelp.

2 TO PREPARE MARINADE: Combine marinade ingredients and use to marinate the dried kelp and slimy mackerel.

3 Half fill the oshi-zushi container with rice. Layer the marinated kelp over the rice to completely cover. Place another layer of sushi rice on top of the kelp.

4 Arrange the sliced mackerel over the rice. Using the lid from the oshi-zushi container, press firmly down onto the mackerel.

5 Lift off the lid and remove the frame. You will have a square piece of battera-zushi.

6 Using a sharp knife cut the battera-zushi into 5 cm (2 in) squares and serve.

SERVES 2 TO 4

SCATTERED SUSHI (CHIRASHI-ZUSHI)

This consists simply of a variety of sushi sliced fish arranged over a bed of sushi rice and sprinkled with toasted sesame seeds.
A selection of vegetables is usually arranged with the fish.

Scattered Sushi

Sushi can be made using Western ingredients in place of Japanese ingredients. Western-style sushi are known as yoshoku-zushi. Suitable ingredients include smoked ham, roast beef, raw meat, salami, frankfurters, cheese, canned anchovies and olives.

SILK SQUARE SUSHI (CHAKIN-ZUSHI)

2 cups (10 oz/315 g) sushi rice

50 g (2 oz) pickled ginger (gari)

½ cucumber, thinly sliced

1 teaspoon sesame seeds, toasted

2 Japanese mushrooms, chopped

1 tablespoon green peas

100 g (3 oz) cooked, shelled prawns (shrimps)

5 thin Japanese omelettes (see p. 74)

5 thin, long strips cucumber peel

1 Combine sushi rice, pickled ginger, cucumber, sesame seeds, Japanese mushrooms, green peas and prawns in a bowl.

2 Divide the sushi rice mixture into 5. Place 1 portion of the rice mixture into the centre of an omelette and bring the sides up and around the filling to form a pouch. Tie the ends with cucumber peel.

3 Repeat the process until all 5 chakin-zushi are completed.

SERVES 5

BEAN CURD ROLL (INARI-ZUSHI)

Inari may be purchased cooked or uncooked. The first recipe uses precooked. To cook inari, follow the second recipe.

RECIPE 1

5 inari (bean curd bags), precooked

1 cup (5 oz/155 g) sushi rice

2 tablespoons sesame seeds, toasted

1 Cut each inari in half. Open the halved inari to form a pocket and place a ball of sushi rice inside. Sprinkle the rice with toasted sesame seeds and press the inari openings closed with the fingers.

2 Repeat this process until all the inari are used.

3 TO SERVE: Place on a plate, cut side down. To make inari-zushi look more interesting, they may be tied with thin strips of cucumber skin or kampyo (stalks from dried morning glory flowers). The ends of the inari bags may also be tucked underneath to neaten their appearance.

SERVES 5

RECIPE 2

½ cup (4 fl oz/125 ml) soy sauce

1½ tablespoons mirin wine

½ cup (4 oz/125 g) sugar

¼ cup (2 fl oz/60 ml) water or dashi

5 inari

1 Combine ingredients and place over a low heat. Immerse inari in the hot liquid and cook on low for 30 minutes.

2 Remove inari from liquid and drain.

3 Allow to cool, then use as instructed above.

SERVES 5

ROLLED OMELETTE (FUTO-MAKI)

This recipe is similar to kobana-maki (p. 20) except that the size and shape differ — futo-maki are larger rounds. This is a Tokyo-style recipe. For Osaka style, spinach leaves and local vegetables are added to the filling before it is rolled up, and the sushi rice is sweetened.

3 cups (15 oz/470 g) sushi rice

½ cucumber

50 g (2 oz) pickled ginger

2 sheets dried seaweed

2 small, thin Japanese omelettes (see p. 74)

1 tablespoon wasabi

1 tablespoon sesame seeds, toasted

2 pieces pickled radish (taku-an)

1 Combine the rice, cucumber and ginger.
2 Place 1 slice of seaweed on a bamboo mat. Lay 1 omelette over the seaweed and place half the rice on top. Spread half the wasabi over the rice and sprinkle with half the sesame seeds. Finally place 1 piece of pickled radish on top of the sesame seeds.

3 Using both hands, gently roll the bamboo mat to form a fat cylinder. Using a sharp knife cut into large rounds. Repeat the process using remaining ingredients.
4 Arrange futo-maki on a plate and serve.

SERVES 2 TO 4

*Rolled Omelette and
Cucumber Roll*

SASHIMI

SLICED RAW SEAFOOD

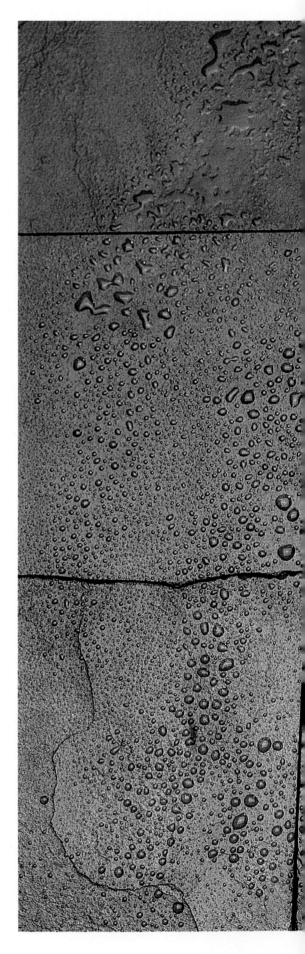

Sashimi is in many ways the very soul of Japanese cuisine. It is served at every formal meal — always early so that the palate has not been dulled by the more obvious flavour of cooked food — and displays the skills of the chef in choosing the best and freshest fish, and in knifework and presentation.

The most crucial step is choosing the fish. It cannot be emphasised too much that it must be the very freshest available. Frozen seafood is definitely not suitable for sashimi. In Japan the fish is often killed and bled just before being cut and served as sashimi.

Presentation is also extremely important. A finished platter of sashimi should look as delicate and beautiful as it tastes. Accompanying dipping sauces should be light, tangy and freshly made.

Fine, lean beef, either chopped or thinly sliced, can also be served raw, sashimi style. All sashimi is served with soy sauce and wasabi (green mustard) and with either thin shreds of horseradish (tsuma) or cucumber and shredded vegetables.

Dancing Green Prawns

STEP-BY-STEP TECHNIQUES

1 *Remove hard beak.*

2 *Take out innards.*

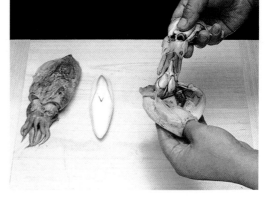

3 *Peel skin away from flesh.*

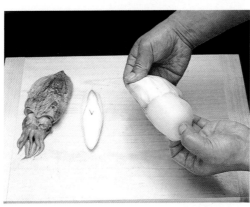

Cuttlefish

CUTTLEFISH (IKA)

3 cuttlefish

½ sheet dried seaweed

¼ teaspoon wasabi

1 x 7½ cm (2½ in) piece spring onion stalk

1 tablespoon pickled ginger

¼ cup (1 oz/30 g) grated horseradish, to garnish

fresh basil seeds, to garnish

1 Clean and skin the cuttlefish following illustrations below. Then, using a sharp knife, hold the cuttlefish flat on a board and carefully run the knife through it leaving a join at the end. Open out to give 2 thin fillets, butterfly style, about the same size from each cuttlefish.

2 Lay the seaweed over one half of the opened-out cuttlefish. Place wasabi, spring onion stalk and pickled ginger over the seaweed. Fold over other half of cuttlefish to cover.

3 Carefully roll cuttlefish into a cylinder and cut into 1 cm (½ in) rounds. Arrange cuttlefish rounds on a plate and serve garnished with horseradish and some fresh basil seeds.

SERVES 2 TO 3

CRISPY CARP IN ICED WATER (KOI-NO-ARAI)

In Japan live jewfish is more commonly used than carp (see below). The fish is cut at the back of the head so the blood escapes, leaving the flesh clean and crisp. The fish must be eaten as soon as it is taken from the iced water.

2 live carp

iced water

GARNISH

soy sauce

wasabi

lemon slices

1 Clean and fillet the carp.
2 Slice the fillets thinly, sashimi style, and plunge immediately into ice-cold water for 5 minutes. This will shrink and crisp the flesh.
3 Remove fish from the water and arrange on a serving plate. Serve accompanied by soy sauce, wasabi and lemon slices.

SERVES 2

OCTOPUS (TAKO)

1 medium-sized octopus

½ cup (4 oz/125 g) salt

4 cups (32 fl oz/1 litre) water

¼ cup (2 fl oz/60 ml) vinegar

iced water

50 g (2 oz) fresh, tender seaweed, shredded, to serve

sweet and sour vinegar, optional

1 Rub whole octopus with the salt to remove all sliminess.
2 Place water and vinegar in saucepan and bring to the boil.
3 Holding octopus by its tentacles gently dip it in and out of the water three times. This will stabilise the skin colour and prevent skin from splitting. Then carefully place the octopus in the water and cook for 4 minutes on high heat, turning occasionally. Continue to cook for a further 3 minutes on medium heat.
4 Remove from hot liquid and plunge into ice-cold water, so it shrinks and cools at the same time. Remove from cold water, turn the head inside out and remove all the guts. Clean head thoroughly and turn right side out.
5 To serve, the octopus can be diced or thinly sliced sashimi style or marinated in sweet and sour vinegar (sunomono) for 1 hour beforehand. Serve on a bed of shredded seaweed.

SERVES 4

CRISPY JEWFISH IN ICED WATER (SUZUKI-NO-ARAI)

Suzuki-no-ari is prepared using a live jewfish, cut at the back of the head and bled as in the recipe for Crispy Carp above.

1 small, live jewfish

iced water

GARNISH

soy sauce

wasabi

lemon wedges

1 Clean and fillet the jewfish.
2 Quickly slice the fish thinly, sashimi style. Then plunge immediately into ice-cold water for 5 minutes to shrink and crisp the fish.
3 Serve and eat as soon as possible accompanied by soy sauce, wasabi and lemon wedges.

SERVES 2 TO 3

STEP-BY-STEP TECHNIQUES

1 *Shell prawns and remove heads and tails.*

2 *Slice down back and devein.*

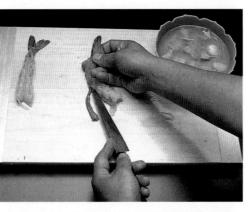

3 *Cut flesh into 1¼ cm (½ in) pieces.*

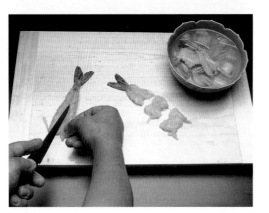

DANCING GREEN PRAWNS (ODORI)

This method of preparation is similar to that used in the Crispy Carp and Crispy Jewfish recipes (see p.29).

5 live green tiger prawns (shrimps)
400 g (13 oz) ice cubes or party ice

SEAWEED ROLL
1 large green tiger prawn (shrimp)
1 sheet dried seaweed

GARNISH
½ lemon, sliced
1 small carrot, shredded
100 g (3 oz) daikon, shredded
5 cucumber rounds, thinly sliced
1 dessertspoon wasabi
soy sauce, optional

1 Cut heads and tails off the 5 prawns and set aside. Remove shells and chop flesh into 1¼ cm (½ in) pieces. Mix flesh into the ice and allow to stand for 5 minutes.

2 TO PREPARE THE SEAWEED ROLL: Peel single prawn completely and chop flesh. Spread prawn flesh over the sheet of dried seaweed and roll up tightly. Cut into 2½ cm (1 in) lengths.

3 Arrange the head and tail of each prawn on an individual serving plate. Place a portion of the iced flesh alongside the head and garnish with lemon slices, seaweed roll, shredded carrot and daikon, sliced cucumber and wasabi. Soy sauce may be served separately in a small shallow bowl.

SERVES 5

LIVE GREEN LOBSTER (ISEEBI-NO-IKEZUKURI)

It is essential to use a live fresh lobster to obtain the correct texture for this dish. Frozen lobster flesh becomes rubbery, dry and tough and is not suitable for eating raw. All types of lobster are suitable for iseebi-no-ikezukuri as long as they are very fresh.

1 medium-sized live green lobster
400 g (13 oz) ice cubes or party ice
100 g (3 oz) horseradish, shredded
lemon slices, to garnish
½ tablespoon wasabi, to garnish
soy sauce

SEAWEED ROLL
1 sheet dried seaweed
1 small cucumber, thinly sliced in strips
100 g (3 oz) fresh tuna, sliced sashimi style

1 Insert a sharp knife through the lobster flesh where the tail meets the head. Carefully separate the head and tail from the lobster. Remove brain and serve separately. Gently remove lobster meat from the tail shell and head and chop into 2½ cm (1 in) pieces.
2 Place lobster pieces into a bowl and mix in the ice. Allow to stand for 5 minutes to make the flesh crisp.
3 Remove flesh from the ice and replace in shell. Arrange lobster on a bed of shredded horseradish on a long serving platter.
4 TO PREPARE SEAWEED ROLL: Arrange cucumber strips to cover the seaweed. Layer the tuna over cucumber and roll up tightly to form a long cylinder. Cut into 2½ cm (1 in) pieces.
5 Serve the lobster garnished with the seaweed rolls, lemon slices and wasabi and accompanied by soy sauce.

SERVES 2

Live Green Lobster

CHOPPED BEEF (NIKU-NO-TATAKI)

Beef sashimi is also popular in Japan today despite the high price of beef. It is simple to prepare and delicious to eat.

1 x 300 g (10 oz) piece eye fillet of beef
shredded cucumber or grated horseradish, to garnish

MARINADE
2 cups (16 fl oz/500 ml) white vinegar
½ cup (4 oz/125 g) sugar
2 spring onions, finely chopped
2 cm (¾ in) piece green ginger, grated

1 Thinly slice beef and then cut into small squares.
2 TO PREPARE MARINADE: Combine vinegar, sugar, spring onions and ginger in a bowl and marinate meat in this mixture for a few seconds.
3 Remove beef from marinade and serve on a platter accompanied by shredded cucumber or grated horseradish.

SERVES 2

Salt-grilled Bonito

SALT-GRILLED BONITO (KATSUO-NO-TATAKI)

Bonito is naturally a strongly flavoured fish but prepared in this way it has quite a subtle flavour.

1 medium-sized bonito (katsuo)

3 tablespoons salt

iced water

1 onion, thinly sliced into rings

1 dried red chilli, chopped

1 tablespoon finely chopped seaweed

1 Fillet bonito and discard head, tail and bones. Skewer fillets lengthways, skin side up, in 2 or 3 places. Cover skin with a layer of salt and grill on high heat for 2 minutes. Remove from griller and plunge into ice-cold water for a minute or so.

2 While the fish is immersed in the water, rub the salt from the skin and remove skewers. Take bonito fillets from the water and cut each fillet in 2 lengthways. Remove any large bones from the fish and slice it sashimi style.

3 Arrange fish on a serving plate.

4 Combine onion rings with chilli and seaweed and spread over the sliced fish.

SERVES 2

SLICED BEEF (NIKU-NO-SASHIMI)

Although raw meat is commonly eaten in Japan it has only recently become acceptable in the West.
Niku-no-sashimi is a simple dish to prepare and lends itself to entertaining either small or large groups of people without undue fuss.

1 fresh eye fillet of beef

GARNISH

soy sauce

wasabi

spring onions, chopped

1 Using a very sharp knife, slice beef thinly, sushi style. The eye fillet may be frozen for one hour prior to slicing in order to obtain the thinnest possible slices.

2 To serve niku-no-sashimi, arrange beef slices decoratively on a serving dish. For variation in presentation, the slices may be moulded into the shape of a flower.

3 Niki-no-sashimi is served with soy sauce, wasabi and chopped spring onions. Strongly flavoured dipping sauces and vegetables are not served as they may mask the subtle flavour of the raw beef.

SERVES 4

STEP-BY-STEP TECHNIQUES

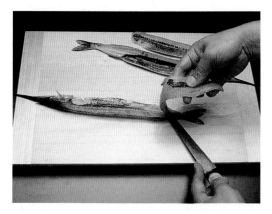

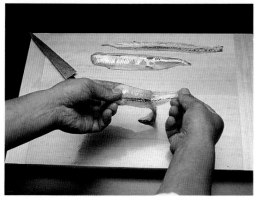

1 *Using a long-bladed fish knife, cut into fish below head and carefully slice a long fillet off backbone.*

2 *Turn fish over and cut a similar fillet from other side.*

3 *Peel skin from fillets.*

GARFISH (SAYORI)

3 medium-sized garfish
dipping sauce, optional

GARNISH
3 prawns (shrimps)
wasabi
lemon slices

1 Clean, fillet and skin the garfish, discarding head, tail and bones as illustrated in the step-by-step photographs. Once each garfish is filleted into 2 pieces, cut down the centre of each fillet so you have 4 fillets. (It is important when cutting down the centre of the fillets that you cut in the middle of the stripe marked on the flesh.)

2 Using the fingers, roll each fillet into a snail shape, ensuring that the stripe on the flesh is facing upwards. The two-toned fish fillet looks beautiful when presented in this way. As an alternative to this method of presentation, each fillet can be tied into a loose knot.

3 To serve sayori, arrange each fillet on a plate and garnish with a prawn, wasabi and thin lemon slices. Sayori may also be accompanied by a favourite dipping sauce.

SERVES 3

Garfish Sashimi

WHOLE SNAPPER (SUGATA-ZUKURI)

In Japan sugata-zukuri is a popular dish for special occasions such as weddings and similar joyous celebrations.

1 medium-sized whole snapper
1 lemon

1 Clean, scale and fillet the snapper into 2 large pieces. Remove skin from only 1 of the fillets. Slice the skinned fillet sashimi style.

2 Place a piece of kitchen paper on the skin side of the remaining fillet and pour boiling water over it. This method is called shimo-furi and removes excess oiliness from the fish. Remove the paper and slice fillet with the skin still on into sashimi slices.

3 Sugata-zukuri means whole snapper, so on presentation of this dish, the head, tail and bones are used as a bed on which the sashimi sliced flesh is arranged. The lemon is sliced and arranged between the pieces of snapper, not only as a garnish but to give additional flavour to the dish.

Whole Snapper

SERVES 4

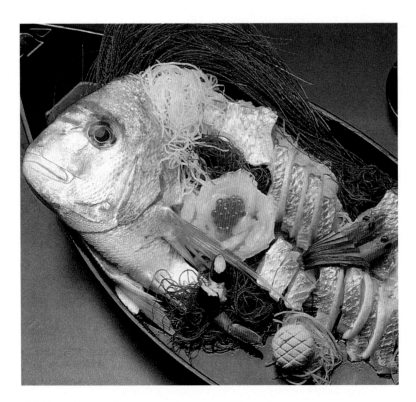

CHOPPED YELLOWTAIL (AJI-NO-TATAKI)

5 medium-sized fresh whole yellowtail

MARINADE
2 cups (16 fl oz/500 ml) white vinegar
½ cup (4 oz/125 g) sugar
2 spring onion stalks, finely chopped
2 cm (¾ in) piece green ginger, grated

1 Clean, scale and fillet the yellowtail and remove skin and bones. Chop flesh into small dice.

2 TO PREPARE MARINADE: Combine vinegar, sugar, shallots and ginger in a bowl and marinate fish in this mixture for 10 seconds.

3 Remove fish from marinade and using the back of a knife flatten the fish slightly. Serve with head, tail and bones as in recipe for Whole Snapper.

SERVES 5

TUNA FISH (MAGURO)

300 g (10 oz) fresh tuna
horseradish, shredded

DIPPING SAUCE
1 tablespoon wasabi
2 tablespoons soy sauce
basil seeds, optional

1 Slice tuna thinly, sashimi style.

2 Place shredded horseradish on a serving plate. Arrange slices of tuna over the horseradish.

3 TO PREPARE DIPPING SAUCE: Mix together the wasabi and soy sauce. Basil seeds can be added to the sauce for extra flavour.

4 Serve the tuna accompanied by the dipping sauce.

SERVES 4

DIPPING SAUCES

SESAME SAUCE (GOMA-DARE)

170 g (6 oz) white sesame seeds

1 cup (8 fl oz/250 ml) soy sauce

4 tablespoons mirin wine

2 tablespoons sugar

1½ cups (12 fl oz/360 ml) dashi

1 cup (5 oz/155 g) spring onions, finely chopped

2 cups (10 oz/315 g) daikon, finely grated

1 Dry-fry sesame seeds, taking care not to burn them.
2 Using a pestle and mortar, grind seeds to a paste. Transfer to a bowl.
3 Mix in soy sauce, mirin, sugar and dashi.
4 Just before serving, add chopped spring onions and grated daikon, and stir well to combine.

YIELDS ABOUT 5 CUPS (40 FL OZ/1¼ LITRES)

SOY SAUCE WITH HORSERADISH (WASABI-JOYU)

1 cup (8 fl oz/250 ml) soy sauce

1 tablespoon mirin wine

3 tablespoons horseradish, chopped

Combine all ingredients in a bowl shortly before serving.

YIELDS ABOUT 1½ CUPS (12 FL OZ/360 ML)

SOY SAUCE WITH GINGER (SHOGA-JOYU)

1 cup (8 fl oz/250 ml) soy sauce

3 tablespoons chopped fresh ginger root, or more, to taste

Combine ingredients in a bowl shortly before serving.

YIELDS ABOUT 1 CUP (8 FL OZ/250 ML)

SOY SAUCE WITH SESAME SEEDS (GOMA-JOYU)

3 tablespoons white sesame seeds, dry-fried and ground into paste

1 cup (8 fl oz/250 ml) soy sauce

Combine soy sauce and sesame paste in a bowl shortly before serving.

YIELDS ABOUT 1 CUP (8 FL OZ/250 ML)

SOY SAUCE WITH PICKLED PLUMS (BAINIKU-JOYU)

1 cup (8 fl oz/250 ml) soy sauce

1 tablespoon mirin wine

½ cup (3 oz/90 g) canned pickled plums, or more, to taste

1 Combine liquid ingredients in a bowl.
2 Purée pickled plums and stir into sauce mixture.

YIELDS ABOUT 1½ CUPS (12 FL OZ/360 ML)

PONZU SAUCE

This sauce can be stored in the refrigerator for up to one year.

¾ cup (6 fl oz/180 ml) rice vinegar

2 cups (16 fl oz/500 ml) soy sauce

2 cups (16 fl oz/500 ml) fresh lemon juice, strained

½ cup (4 fl oz/125 ml) mirin wine

2 cups (16 fl oz/500 ml) dashi

Combine ingredients in bowl and leave for at least 24 hours before using.

YIELDS 6 CUPS (48 FL OZ/1½ LITRES)

DEEP-FRIED FOODS

AGE-MONO AND TEMPURA

There are several methods of Japanese-style deep frying, the best known of which is tempura — batter-coated deep frying. There are tempura bars and restaurants throughout Japan where these dishes are cooked to perfection. But they are, for all their delicacy, fairly easy to cook in an average kitchen. The oil for frying should be very light — polyunsaturated vegetable oil is best — and perfectly clean. A few drops of sesame oil can be added for flavour if liked.

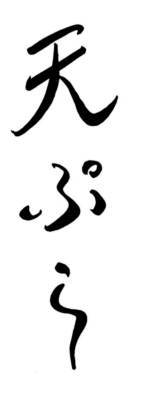

Deep-fried Cuttlefish

2 Coat the seasoned fillets in plain flour, dip into the beaten egg yolks, then coat with breadcrumbs, pressing firmly into the pork.
3 Heat the oil. Fry crumbed pork fillets until golden. Remove and drain on kitchen paper. Slice each fillet neatly and arrange on a bed of finely shredded cabbage or simply garnish with fine shreds of dried seaweed.
4 Tonkatsu sauce and mustard are used as dipping sauces to accompany the pork.

SERVES 2

LEMON SOLE WITH SAUCE (HIRAME NO-ANKAKE)

3 medium-sized lemon sole
oil for deep frying

SAUCE
½ cup (2 oz/60 g) cornflour
½ cup (4 fl oz/125 ml) soy sauce
½ tablespoon mirin wine
½ cup (4 fl oz/125 ml) dashi
pinch salt
1 tablespoon grated ginger
250 g (8 oz) bean curd, diced
spring onions, chopped
lemon slices, to garnish
cucumber peel, in strips, to garnish

1 Clean and scale the sole. Using a sharp knife cut down the middle of the sole through to the bone. Then make a cut at right angles, along base of head. Gently lift and roll the flesh outwards on both sides exposing the backbone.
2 Heat oil, carefully slide fish in and cook until crisp and golden brown. Remove from oil and drain. Repeat with remaining lemon sole. Keep sole warm.
3 TO PREPARE SAUCE: Combine the cornflour, soy sauce, mirin, dashi and salt. Place in a saucepan and simmer over gentle heat until thick. Squeeze juice from grated

Deep Fried Pork Fillets

DEEP-FRIED PORK FILLETS (TONKATSU)

If deep frying, ½ cup (4 fl oz/125 ml) of sesame oil may be added for extra flavour.
If Tonkatsu sauce is unavailable substitute Worcestershire sauce, or make up a mixture of 1 tablespoon sugar, ¼ cup (2 fl oz/60 ml) tomato sauce, 1 teaspoon soy sauce and a sprinkling of nutmeg and paprika.

600 g (1 lb 4 oz) pork fillet, cut into ½ cm (¼ in) thick slices lengthways
salt and pepper
¾ cup (3 oz/100 g) plain flour
8 egg yolks, beaten
1¾ cups (7 oz/220 g) breadcrumbs
1 tablespoon oil
1 cup (8 fl oz/250 ml) Tonkatsu sauce (bottled)
mustard
cabbage or dried seaweed, finely shredded, to garnish

1 Flatten each fillet with a mallet. Sprinkle with salt and pepper and allow to stand for 5 minutes.

ginger and add to the sauce. Gently combine the sauce with the diced bean curd and chopped spring onions.

4 Arrange the fish on plates and pour the sauce into the opening of each lemon sole. Garnish with lemon slices and a strip of cucumber peel.

SERVES 3 TO 4

DEEP-FRIED GARFISH (SAYORI NANBAN-ZUKE)

5 medium-sized garfish

oil for deep frying

horseradish, grated, to garnish

1 lemon, thinly sliced, to garnish

MARINADE

2 cups (16 fl oz/500 ml) white vinegar

2½ tablespoons sugar

pinch salt

3 tablespoons mirin wine

5 whole dried red chillies

1 onion, sliced

1 spring onion stalk, chopped

1 Clean, scale and gut garfish. Pass a skewer through each garfish beginning at the tail and finishing at the head so that it forms an S-shape.

2 Heat the oil. Drop each fish into hot oil and fry until golden and crisp. Remove from oil and drain.

3 TO PREPARE MARINADE: Combine the vinegar, sugar, salt, mirin, whole chillies, onion and spring onion in a bowl. Marinate the fried garfish in this sweet and sour sauce for 1 hour to allow the flavours to penetrate the flesh.

4 Remove fish from marinade and arrange on serving dish. Garnish with the vegetables from the marinade as well as some grated horseradish and thin lemon slices.

SERVES 5

DEEP-FRIED CHICKEN (TATSUTA-AGE)

200 g (7 oz) chicken breasts, filletted and cut into 5 cm (2 in) squares

1 sheet dried seaweed (nori), finely chopped

½ cup (2 oz/60 g) cornflour

oil for deep frying

hot English mustard

MARINADE

½ cup (4 fl oz/125 ml) soy sauce

¼ cup (2 fl oz/60 ml) mirin wine

pinch salt

pinch ground basil

1 TO PREPARE MARINADE: Combine soy sauce, mirin, salt and basil. Place chicken pieces into marinade and leave for 10 minutes. Remove chicken from marinade and drain.

2 Heat the oil. Mix the the seaweed with the cornflour. Roll each piece of chicken in the cornflour, coating evenly. Deep fry chicken until golden. Drain.

3 Serve on a plate accompanied by hot English mustard.

SERVES 2 TO 3

Lemon Sole with Sauce

BEEF KEBABS (MEAT KUSHI-AGE)

This is a modern Japanese-style dish, very good for parties. Fish is a good substitute for the beef and can be served in the same way.

200 g (7 oz) eye fillet of beef, thinly sliced
100 g (3 oz) Cheddar cheese
2 spring onion stalks
1 carrot

BATTER
100 g (3 oz) plain flour
2 egg yolks, beaten
1 packet Japanese breadcrumbs
oil for deep frying
Tongkatsu sauce or yellow mustard soy sauce, to serve

1 Cut cheese and spring onions into 7 cm (2½ in) lengths. Cut carrot into 7 cm (2½ in) julienne strips and blanch in boiling water until tender.

2 Place a piece of cheese, spring onion and carrot into the centre of a slice of fillet and roll up tightly. Secure each roll with bamboo skewers.

Fish Kebabs

3 Heat the oil.

4 TO PREPARE BATTER: Combine flour with egg yolks. Dip each roll into the batter and then coat with breadcrumbs. Deep fry each roll until centre is cooked and outside browned. Remove from oil and drain.

5 Using a sharp knife cut the rolls into rounds 2½ cm (1 in) thick and arrange on a plate. Serve with Tongkatsu sauce or with yellow mustard and soy sauce.

SERVES 2 TO 3

DEEP-FRIED CALAMARI (IKA)

1 calamari (squid)
1 tablespoon sesame seeds
1 spring onion stalk, finely chopped
oil for deep frying

BATTER
2 egg yolks
2 cups (16 fl oz/500 ml) iced water
2 cups (8 oz/250 g) plain flour

GARNISH
lemon slices
carrot, grated
seaweed, shredded

1 Clean and skin the squid as shown for cuttlefish (p. 28). Use a sharp knife to cut the squid tube into rings.

2 TO PREPARE BATTER: In a bowl combine the egg yolks, water and flour using chopsticks. Allow to rest 5 minutes. Add the sesame seeds, chopped spring onions and squid rings to the batter and mix.

3 Heat oil and, using chopsticks, place 5 or 6 rings into the oil at a time. When golden remove from the oil and drain.

4 Serve, skewered on Japanese folded rice paper garnished with lemon, carrot and seaweed.

SERVES 2 TO 3

DRESSED-UP PRAWNS (KESYO-AGE)

5 large green prawns (shrimps)

1¼ cups (5 oz/150 g) coarse rice flour (domyoji)

1 sheet dried seaweed, cut into 5 small pieces

oil for deep frying

BATTER

1 egg yolk, beaten

1 cup (8 fl oz/250 ml) iced water

1 cup (4 oz/125 g) plain flour

GARNISH

deep-fried seaweed bow

ginger, grated

horseradish

1 Shell and devein the prawns. Make 4 incisions into the undersection of each prawn and open up the cuts to straighten.

2 TO PREPARE BATTER: Combine batter ingredients in a bowl. Wrap a small piece of seaweed around the end of the prawn tail and dip each prawn into the batter. Do not coat the seaweed nor the tail with the batter.

3 Coat the prawns with rice flour.

4 Heat oil and fry prawns until light golden in colour. Remove from oil and drain.

5 Arrange prawns in a dish on a folded sheet of rice paper. Garnish with a deep fried seaweed bow, grated ginger and horseradish.

SERVES 2 TO 3

DEEP-FRIED WHOLE TROUT (MASU NANBAN-ZUKE)

3 whole trout

oil for deep frying

MARINADE

2 cups (16 fl oz/500 ml) white vinegar

2½ tablespoons sugar

pinch salt

Dressed-up Prawns

3 tablespoons mirin wine

5 whole dried red chillies

1 onion, sliced

1 spring onion stalk, chopped

GARNISH

dried red chillies

1 onion, sliced

horseradish, grated

green leaves

1 Clean, scale and remove backbone from each trout. Thread trout onto skewers, shaping to form an S.

2 Heat the oil. Fry each trout until golden and crisp. Remove from oil and drain.

3 TO PREPARE MARINADE: Combine the vinegar, sugar, salt, mirin, whole chillies, sliced onion and chopped spring onion in a bowl. Marinate the fried fish in this sweet and sour sauce for 1 hour, to allow flavours to penetrate the flesh.

4 Remove fish from the marinade and arrange on a serving dish. Garnish with chillies, sliced onion, a ball of grated horseradish and green leaves from any flower.

SERVES 3

STEP-BY-STEP TECHNIQUES

PRAWN TEMPURA (EBI)

Prawn tempura is well known throughout the world. The key to a successful ebi is short, intense cooking — overcooking causes toughness. Ebi must be full of flavour, crisp on the outside and tender inside. Ebi is sometimes served with lemon and salt. A tempura sauce and grated horseradish may also accompany this dish.

5 large green prawns (shrimps)

1 sheet dried seaweed, cut into 5 small pieces

flour for coating

oil for deep frying

BATTER

1 cup (4 oz/125 g) plain flour

1 cup (8 fl oz/250 ml) iced water

1 egg yolk, beaten

Prawn Tempura

1 *Combine flour, egg yolk and iced water to make batter.*

2 *Dip each prawn in flour, then in batter.*

3 *Drop into hot oil.*

4 *Fry until golden, remove and drain.*

1 Shell and devein prawns. Cut 4 incisions into the undersection of each prawn and straighten them out to open up the cuts. Tie a piece of seaweed around the base of the tail. Coat each prawn with flour, leaving the seaweed and tail uncoated.

2 Heat the oil.

3 TO PREPARE BATTER: Combine flour, water and yolk. Dip each prawn into the batter (leaving seaweed and tail uncoated) and slip into the hot oil. Fry until golden, remove and drain. Arrange on rice paper and serve.

SERVES 2

NOODLE COATED PRAWNS (EBI NO-SOMEN)

5 large green prawns (shrimps)

oil for deep frying

2 small bunches somen noodles

1 small piece dried seaweed

dipping sauce

sliced lemon, to garnish

BATTER

2 egg yolks

2 cups (16 fl oz/500 ml) iced water

2 cups (8 oz/250 g) plain flour

1 Shell and devein prawns. Make a shallow incision into the underside of prawns and open up the cuts to straighten them.

2 TO PREPARE BATTER: Place egg yolks, flour and water in a bowl and blend together using chopsticks.

3 Heat oil. Place noodles on a board.

4 Dip each prawn into the batter and press into the somen so they adhere to and cover the prawn. Wrap a 2 cm (¾ in) strip of seaweed around the centre of the prawn and gently slide into the hot oil. Cook until noodles are golden brown and serve hot.

5 Arrange on a plate and serve with a dipping sauce and lemon garnish.

SERVES 2 TO 3

1 *Roll each battered prawn in somen.*

2 *Press somen onto prawn so they adhere.*

3 *Wrap a strip of seaweed round centre of each prawn.*

4 *Drop into hot oil, fry until golden and drain.*

POT COOKING

Japanese pot-cooked dishes are tasty, fairly substantial and warming. They make a satisfying country-style meal in the tradition of the daubes of provincial France and the stews of the British Isles.

But there the resemblance ends. Instead of long, slow cooking in the European tradition, small morsels of food are cooked very quickly in a steaming pot of broth. A small charcoal brazier or spirit burner keeps the pot bubbling at the table and diners select pieces of food from artistically arranged dishes of meat, fish, chicken and vegetables. These are dipped into the pot with chopsticks to cook briefly. The broth may be served separately in bowls at the end of the meal.

When preparing ingredients for pot-cooked dishes, cut food into small pieces so it will cook quickly. Vegetables should predominate over animal protein; this is nutritionally sound and looks more decorative on a platter.

Sukiyaki

NOODLE SAUCE (TSUKEJIRU)

1 cup (8 fl oz/250 ml) soy sauce

5 tablespoons mirin wine

3½ cups (28 fl oz/850 ml) dashi

1 tablespoon sugar

1 Place soy sauce, mirin, dashi and sugar in a small pan. Heat until just boiling.

2 Allow to cool, then transfer to an airtight container and refrigerate. Stores well for several months.

YIELDS ABOUT 5 CUPS (40 FL OZ/1¼ LITRES)

INDIVIDUAL SUKIYAKI NOODLES (NABEYAKI UDON)

675 g (1 lb 5 oz) dried udon noodles

12 small sprigs watercress, washed and dried

6 fresh mushrooms, thinly sliced

6 green prawns (shrimps), shelled and deveined

6 cups (48 fl oz/1½ litres) noodle broth

6 eggs

1 Cook noodles following the instructions on the packet. Drain and rinse in cold water.

2 Simmer noodle broth (see recipe below) gently.

3 In 6 individual heatproof dishes with lids, make layers of noodles, followed by watercress, mushrooms and prawns. Add 1 cup (8 fl oz/250 ml) noodle broth to each dish, cover and boil for 5 minutes.

4 Make a small well in the centre of each serving and carefully break an egg into it. Replace lid and cook gently until egg is just cooked.

SERVES 6

BUCKWHEAT NOODLES (ZARU SOBA)

350 g (11 oz) dried buckwheat noodles (soba)

4 cups (32 fl oz/1 litre) noodle sauce

CONDIMENTS

⅔ cup (4 oz/125 g) finely shredded spring onions

1½ teaspoons finely grated wasabi

2 tablespoons finely grated ginger root

Cook noodles in a large saucepan of boiling water, taking care not to overcook. Run under cold water, then drain. Serve with chopsticks. Noodles are dipped into sauce and are served with tasty garnishes. The condiments can be added to the sauce for extra flavour.

SERVES 6

NOODLE BROTH (KAKE-JIRU)

Use your favourite soy sauce. There are many different kinds available, and your choice will affect the flavour of the broth.

6 cups (48 fl oz/1½ litre) dashi

2 tablespoons mirin wine

4 tablespoons soy sauce

2 tablespoons sugar

1 Combine all broth ingredients in a saucepan, stir well and bring to the boil. Lower heat, and keep simmering until ready to use.

2 This broth can be stored in the refrigerator for several days.

YIELDS ABOUT 6 CUPS (48 FL OZ/1½ LITRES)

Step-by-Step Techniques

SUKIYAKI

600 g eye (1 lb 4 oz) fillet or scotch fillet, thinly sliced

4 spring onions, cut into 7½ cm (2½ in) lengths

½ Japanese cabbage, sliced into 5 cm (2 in) pieces

2 bamboo shoots, thinly sliced

1 carrot, finely shredded

125 g (4 oz) bean curd, cut into 2½ cm (1 in) squares

100 g (3 oz) suet, cut into long, thin pieces

3 Japanese mushrooms (shiitake), soaked in warm water for about 20 minutes

100 g (3 oz) rice noodles, soaked in warm water for 30 minutes

4 spinach leaves or watercress sprigs, rolled and cut into 7½ cm (2½ in) lengths

2 baby corn cobs, cut in half

some Japanese hill vegetables (carrots, mushrooms, daikon, etc), cut in shapes

3 raw eggs, beaten (optional)

saké or water (optional)

SAUCE (WARISHITA)

1 cup (8 fl oz/250 ml) soy sauce

¼ cup (2 fl oz/60 ml) mirin wine

½ cup (4 oz/125 g) sugar

pinch salt

1 piece dried kelp or ½ cup (4 fl oz/125 ml) dashi

1 Form the suet into the shape of a blooming flower, as shown in the illustrations.

2 TO PREPARE THE WARISHITA SAUCE: Combine the soy sauce, mirin, salt and dried kelp (or dashi) in a saucepan and heat for 30 minutes on low heat.

3 Arrange all the ingredients on a plate.

4 Heat a frying pan and place the suet flower in it. Use this to grease the base of the pan. Gently fry the beef and onions. When tender, pour over some of the warishita

sauce, then add remaining ingredients (except the eggs) to the pan. Add the rest of the sauce and cook gently until tender. During the frying process some saké or water may be added to prevent excessive flavour development of the warishita and to maintain a balance of flavours throughout the cooking.

5 To serve sukiyaki, place the beaten eggs in a bowl and use for dipping the sukiyaki pieces into. The raw egg is optional and not always used by Western people. Sukiyaki is served from the pot into small bowls.

SERVES 4

1 *Thinly slice fillet.*

2 *Place suet flower in frypan.*

3 *Add beef pieces and shallots.*

4 *Add remaining ingredients.*

5 *Pour over warishita sauce.*

❖ *Sukiyaki is a world-famous Japanese dish. It can be cooked and served at the table. The many colours in this dish are a treat for the eye and help stimulate the appetite.*

UDON NOODLES IN BROTH (KAKE-UDON)

8 cups (64 fl oz/2 litres) noodle broth (see p. 46)

650 g (1 lb 5 oz) dried udon noodles

6 heaped tablespoons finely shredded spring onions, to garnish

1 Simmer noodle broth over low heat.

2 Cook noodles in boiling water as directed. Rinse well.

3 Place noodles into individual noodle bowls and garnish with spring onions. Cover with noodle broth.

SERVES 6

FISH SUKIYAKI (UOSUKI)

White fish such as Spanish mackerel, snapper, barramundi and jewfish should be used for this dish. Red fish such as bonito and tuna are not suitable.

5 large green king prawns (shrimps)

1 small snapper

1 small flathead

½ small green lobster

5 scallops

5 pipis

5 mussels

5 oysters

1 medium crab, uncooked

5 large leaves Japanese cabbage

¼ bunch spring onions, cut into 7½ cm (2½ in) lengths

250 g (8 oz) bean curd, cut into 2½ cm (1 in) squares

1 cup (8 fl oz/250 ml) dashi

warishita sauce (see p. 47)

3 raw eggs, beaten (optional)

1 Shell, clean and dry the king prawns. Clean, scale and fillet the fish and slice it thinly, sashimi style. Reserve the snapper head. Clean and shell remaining shellfish.

2 Blanch cabbage leaves in boiling water for 2 minutes.

3 Lay a cabbage leaf out flat, place a piece of spring onion and a prawn in the centre and roll up tightly. Cut into 5 cm (2 in) pieces.

4 Carefully arrange all ingredients in the pot, including the snapper head. Pour the cold dashi into the pot followed by the warishita sauce. Place pot over a low flame and cook until seafood is tender.

5 Uosuki is served from the pot accompanied by raw beaten eggs in small bowls.

SERVES 5

SALMON NABE (ISHI KARI-NABE)

Frozen salmon may be substituted if fresh salmon is not available. If using fresh salmon, the head, fins and tail can be reserved and used to make an excellent fish stock.

1 medium-sized salmon

12 Japanese dried mushrooms (shiitake), soaked in warm water for 10 minutes

250 g (8 oz) bean curd, cut into 6 squares

½ Japanese cabbage, coarsely shredded into 5 cm (2 in) wide pieces

2 x 5 cm (2 in) pieces bamboo shoot

8 cups (64 fl oz/2 litres) seasoned dashi

4 tablespoons Japanese soy sauce

¼ cup (2 fl oz/60 ml) mirin wine or saké

pinch salt

dipping sauces, eg Ponzu or sesame sauce

1 Clean and scale salmon. Remove fins, tail and head. Slice into 5 cm (2 in) thick cutlets.

2 Place all ingredients into the pot and add the dashi, soy sauce, mirin or saké and salt. Place over a medium heat and simmer, covered, for 15 minutes.

3 Turn the salmon pieces over and simmer a further 15 minutes or until tender. When cooked, serve salmon in the pot accompanied by a variety of sauces such as sesame or Ponzu (see p. 35).

SERVES 3 TO 4

Fish Sukiyaki

BEEF IN BROTH (SHABU-SHABU)

This is an ideal dinner party dish.

6–8 cups (48–64 fl oz/1½–2 litres) dashi

750 g (1 lb 8 oz) beef or lamb, sliced very thinly

½ small Japanese cabbage, shredded into bite-sized pieces

250 g (8 oz) bamboo shoots, thinly sliced

250 g (8 oz) mushrooms, sliced

½ bunch spring onions, sliced

1 cake bean curd, cut into pieces

dipping sauces, eg Ponzu or sesame sauce

1 Pour dashi into a casserole on a burner or electric wok, and set it up at the dinner table.

2 Arrange remaining ingredients attractively on large serving dishes. Guests help themselves: pieces of vegetable and meat are picked up in chopsticks and dipped in the hot dashi until just cooked.

3 Serve with dipping sauces, such as Ponzu or sesame sauces (see p. 35).

SERVES 4

SUKIYAKI NOODLES (UDON-SUKI)

600 g (1 lb 3 oz) dried udon noodles

150 g (5 oz) daikon, boiled for 10 minutes and cut into 1 cm (½ in) slices

600 g (1 lb 3 oz) chicken meat, cut into 5 cm (2 in) pieces

150 g (5 oz) bamboo shoots, cut into 5 cm (2 in) pieces

4 leaves Japanese cabbage, blanched in boiling water for 1 minute, cut into 5 cm (2 in) pieces

6 spinach leaves, blanched in boiling water for 1 minute, cut into 5 cm (2 in) pieces

10 fresh mushrooms, cut into 5 cm (2 in) pieces

3 cakes bean curd, grilled each side, cut into 5 cm (2 in) pieces

STOCK
10 cups (80 fl oz/2½ litres) dashi

⅔ cup (5½ fl oz/165 ml) soy sauce

⅓ tablespoon mirin wine

CONDIMENTS
lemon wedges

chopped spring onions

finely grated ginger root

1 Cook udon noodles according to packet instructions, and set aside.

2 TO PREPARE STOCK: In a casserole or electric wok at the table, combine stock ingredients. Bring to the boil, lower heat and simmer.

3 Arrange all ingredients over the noodles on a serving platter. At the table, place a little of everything that is on the platter (except noodles) in the casserole to cook for a few minutes.

4 Guests are served a small amount of stock in their bowls, to which they add the condiments of their choice. They then remove food from the casserole and dip it into their bowls before eating. At the end of the meal, the noodles are added to the casserole, heated through and served as a noodle broth.

SERVES 6 TO 8

CHICKEN POT (MIZU-TAKI)

1½ kg (3 lb) chicken, cut into bite-sized pieces

12 cups (96 fl oz/3 litres) dashi

½ cup (4 fl oz/125 ml) mirin wine

½ cup (4 fl oz/125 ml) soy sauce

4 tablespoons sugar

VEGETABLES
250 g (8 oz) bamboo shoots, sliced

3 leeks, sliced

3 carrots, sliced

1 bunch spinach, blanched and chopped

6 shiitake mushrooms, soaked and thinly sliced (see Glossary)

150 g (5 oz) bean curd, grilled and cut into pieces

½ small Japanese cabbage, blanched and chopped

Ponzu sauce (see p. 35), for dipping

1 Place chicken pieces into a saucepan with dashi, mirin, soy sauce and sugar. Bring to the boil, turn down heat and simmer vigorously for 30 minutes, or until chicken is cooked.

2 Remove chicken and set aside. Skim broth and transfer to a casserole or electric wok at the dinner table. Simmer broth.

3 Arrange vegetables and chicken pieces attractively on serving dishes. Add vegetables and chicken to broth and simmer for several minutes until vegetables are cooked but still crisp.

4 Guests remove chicken and vegetables from the casserole with chopsticks and dip food into Ponzu sauce before eating.

SERVES 6 TO 8

Chicken Pot

'RIVERBANK' OYSTER CASSEROLE (KAKI DOTE-NABE)

200 g (6½ oz) miso (red or white, or a combination)

3 tablespoons mirin wine

6 cups (48 fl oz/1½ litres) dashi

10 cm (4 in) piece giant kelp, slashed to release flavour

3 leeks, cut diagonally into 5 cm (2 in) lengths

1 bunch spinach, cut into 5 cm (2 in) lengths

½ Japanese cabbage, cut into 5 cm (2 in) lengths

2 carrots, sliced

500 g (1 lb) oysters (removed from shell or bottled)

noodles, optional

1 Mix together miso, mirin and enough dashi to make a paste. Spread paste evenly inside the rim of a casserole dish. This forms the 'riverbank' which guests push down and dissolve in the stew throughout the meal, as though it were a riverbank sliding into a river.

2 Place the casserole on some form of heat at the table. Add kelp and remaining dashi. Bring to the boil, then reduce to a gentle simmer.

3 Guests add their choice of ingredients to the stock, remembering that the oysters will only need seconds to heat through.

4 Serve with noodles, if desired.

SERVES 8

VEGETABLES WITH BEAN CURD (SANSAI NABE)

Sansai makes use of some of the unusual vegetables which grow in the hills of Japan such as bracken, fungus and golden mushrooms (nameko).

1 spinach leaf, blanched for 2 minutes

5 x 7½ cm (3 in) carrot sticks, cooked until tender

3 Japanese cabbage leaves, blanched for 2 minutes

5 pieces bracken

5 nameko (golden mushrooms)

5 pieces lotus root

5 x 5 cm (2 in) pieces bamboo shoot

5 marron (sweet chestnuts)

250 g (8 oz) bean curd

2 spring onion stalks

4 tablespoons Japanese soy sauce

¼ cup (2 fl oz/60 ml) mirin wine

8 cups (64 fl oz/2 litres) seasoned dashi

finely grated ginger, to serve

Ponzu sauce, to serve

1 Place the spinach leaf and a carrot stick onto a cabbage leaf and then using a bamboo mat, roll up lengthwise and press into a square shape. Cut into 5 cm (2 in) pieces (called hakusai-maki).

2 Arrange all remaining ingredients, including the squares, in a pot. Add the soy sauce, mirin wine and dashi and cover. Simmer gently on low heat for 20 minutes.

3 Sansai can be served with finely grated ginger and Ponzu sauce (see p. 35).

SERVES 5

ONE POT SEAFOOD (CHIRINABE)

2 kg (4 lb) firm white fish (bream or snapper) cut into 5 cm (2 in) chunks

3 leeks, thinly sliced

750 g (1½ lb) mushrooms

½ Japanese cabbage, blanched, refreshed and torn into bite-sized pieces

1½ bunches spinach, prepared as cabbage

2 cakes bean curd, grilled and cut into pieces

BROTH

12 cups (96 fl oz/3 litres) dashi

½ cup (4 fl oz/125 ml) mirin wine

½ cup (4 fl oz/125 ml) soy sauce

4 tablespoons sugar

CONDIMENTS

Ponzu sauce (see p. 35)

sliced spring onions

finely grated ginger

lemon wedges

sufficient steamed white rice for 8

1 Prepare and serve this dish as for Chicken pot (see p. 50), keeping in mind the delicate flesh of the fish and the care required in cooking to retain its succulence.

2 Place condiments and sauces of your choice in individual dipping bowls so that guests may flavour fish to their taste.

3 Finish with steamed white rice and the broth served in individual bowls.

SERVES 8

Vegetables with Bean Curd

GRILLED
AND
PAN-FRIED
FOODS

YAKIMONO AND TEPPAN-YAKI

Yakimono literally means 'grilled things' but also includes pan-fried and oven-baked dishes. The aim of this method of cooking is to achieve a crisp, flavoursome exterior and a moist, tender interior. As with most other categories of Japanese cooking, fish features prominently. Piquant dipping sauces are the best accompaniments.

Teppan-yaki or 'mixed grill' restaurants are popular throughout Japan. Patrons choose their own cuts and watch the chef cook them on a griddle built into the dining table. All types of food are cooked teppan-yaki style.

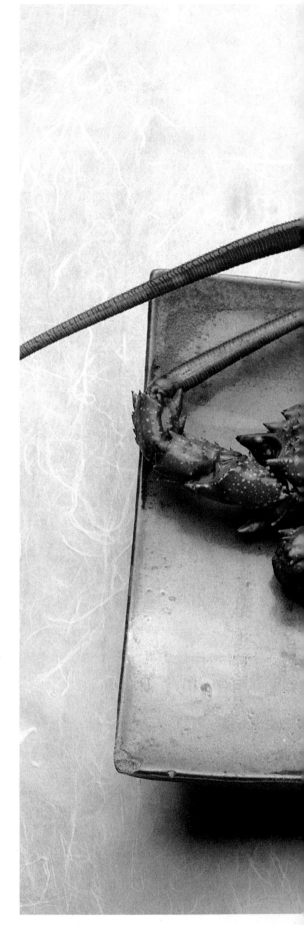

Green Lobster

SNAPPER
(TAI TAKARA-BUNE)

This is a speciality dish in Japan and is popular for celebrations.

1 x 1 kg (2 lb) snapper
1 tablespoon salt
¼ cup (2 fl oz/60 ml) mirin wine
1 mashed sea urchin, optional
2 hard-boiled egg yolks, crumbled
1 tablespoon grated daikon
soy sauce, to serve

1 Clean and scale whole snapper gently, then fillet, leaving bones, head, tail and fins intact. (This filleting method is called sanmai-oroshi meaning 3 pieces — 2 fillets and the skeleton.) Pass a long skewer through the tail and head of the fish so the back is arched or concave. Sprinkle the tail and fins with salt and place under a medium grill until the skeleton sets in the desired concave shape. (This may take up to 30 minutes.) Remove from grill and carefully withdraw the skewer, twisting it slightly to loosen from flesh.

2 Cut each fillet in half widthways and slice into sashimi style slices, keeping the pieces together in order of size. Sprinkle each piece with salt and brush over with the mirin wine. (For an interesting variation, the mirin wine may be combined with a mashed sea urchin before it is brushed onto the fish pieces to add an unusual flavour to the dish.) Place the fish under a moderate grill for 15 minutes, remove and sprinkle with the crumbled yolks and return to grill for a further 2 minutes. Remove fish carefully from grill.

3 Place the fish skeleton onto a serving platter and place a folded sheet of rice paper on it. Arrange the fish pieces neatly over it and serve with the grated daikon and soy sauce.

SERVES 3 TO 4

Snapper

Rainbow Trout

STEAK TERIYAKI
(GYUNIKU TERIYAKI)

600 g (1 lb 3 oz) thin steaks

3 tablespoons vegetable oil

MARINADE

½ cup (4 fl oz/125 ml) soy sauce

½ cup (4 fl oz/125 ml) mirin wine

2 tablespoons sugar

1 teaspoon grated ginger root

1 TO PREPARE MARINADE: combine marinade ingredients and marinate steaks for at least 2 hours. Remove steaks and reserve marinade.

2 In a frying pan, heat the oil and brown steaks for several minutes each side. Remove steaks and set aside.

3 Add reserved marinade to pan juices and stir to combine. Return steaks to pan to heat through briefly.

4 Slice steaks into bite-sized portions. Pour over pan juices and serve with rice.

SERVES 4

RAINBOW TROUT
(MASU)

4 fresh rainbow trout

salt

GARNISH

root ginger, grated or long stemmed pickled ginger

fresh horseradish, grated

soy sauce

lemon wedges

1 Clean, scale and gut trout. Carefully remove the backbone, leaving the head and tail intact. Thread a skewer through the trout and shape into an 'S'. Rub salt onto the skin of the fish and place under a grill at medium heat for 15 minutes. Remove from the grill and withdraw the skewers.

2 Arrange the fish on a plate and serve with grated green ginger, grated horseradish, soy sauce and lemon pieces.

SERVES 4

GREEN LOBSTER OR PRAWNS (ONIGARA-YAKI)

1 whole green lobster or 5 large green tiger prawns (shrimps)

1 tablespoon soy sauce

3 tablespoons mirin wine

2 egg yolks

lemon juice, freshly squeezed

1 teaspoon Japanese dried basil

dried seaweed, sliced or sansho (optional)

1 Cut lobster tail in half. (If using prawns, shell the body, leaving head and tail on. Pass a skewer through the tail to the head to straighten the prawn.)

2 Combine soy sauce, mirin wine and egg yolk and brush over the lobster flesh and tail. (Brush the prawn flesh with the sauce.)

3 Place the lobster or prawns under a grill on medium heat for 15–20 minutes. After grilling, sprinkle with lemon juice.

4 Arrange the seafood on a platter and serve with chopped basil or sansho. Sprinkle with sliced dried seaweed if desired.

SERVES 2

GARFISH (SAYORI NO-SHIO-YAKI)

5 medium-sized garfish

3 tablespoons mirin wine

¼ cup (2 oz/60 g) salt

TO SERVE

daikon, grated or root ginger, grated

soy sauce

1 Clean, scale and gut the garfish. Thread each fish onto bamboo skewers to form an 'S' shape. Sprinkle with the mirin and then with the salt. Place under a moderate grill for 15–20 minutes. Remove from griller and withdraw skewers.

2 Arrange the fish on a plate and serve with grated daikon or green ginger, and soy sauce.

SERVES 5

Garfish

GRILLED CHICKEN YUAN STYLE (TORI NO YUAN-YAKI)

600 g (1 lb 4 oz) boned chicken pieces

3 spring onions, thinly sliced, to garnish

lemon wedges, to serve

MARINADE

½ cup (4 fl oz/125 ml) soy sauce

¾ cup (6 fl oz/180 ml) saké

5 tablespoons mirin wine

1 teaspoon grated ginger root

1 Combine marinade ingredients in a bowl and marinate chicken for an hour.

2 Drain and thread chicken onto skewers. Place under a hot grill and cook each side until golden brown. Remove skewers and cut chicken into small, bite-sized pieces.

3 Garnish with spring onions, and serve with lemon wedges.

SERVES 4

TERIYAKI CHICKEN (TORI NO TERIYAKI)

vegetable oil

3 pieces Chicken Maryland (thigh and drumstick), boned and skin pierced with fork

¾ cup (6 fl oz/180 ml) teriyaki sauce (see following recipe)

ground sansho pepper

1 Heat oil in pan. Cook chicken each side for a few minutes over a moderate heat until golden. Lift chicken from pan and set aside.

2 Add teriyaki sauce to pan juices and bring to the boil. Place chicken back into slightly reduced liquid. Cover and cook for a further 15 minutes on low heat, occasionally basting the chicken with the teriyaki sauce.

3 When the sauce has evaporated, take chicken from the pan and cut into bite-sized pieces.

4 Serve seasoned with sansho pepper.

SERVES 6

TERIYAKI SAUCE

½ cup (4 fl oz/125 ml) soy sauce

2 tablespoons mirin wine

1 tablespoon vegetable oil

1 tablespoon sugar

1 In a pan, combine ingredients and bring to the boil. Stir to dissolve sugar. Remove from heat and use as required.

2 This sauce can be stored in the refrigerator for a few days.

YIELDS ¾ CUP (6 FL OZ/180 ML)

SKEWERED CHICKEN (YAKITORI)

Vegetables and chicken livers can be omitted or other vegetables substituted.

750 g (1 lb 8 oz) chicken meat, boned and cut into 2½ cm (1 in) pieces

350 g (11 oz) chicken livers, halved, rinsed and drained

8 leeks, cut into 2½ cm (1 in) pieces

4 red capsicums (peppers), seeded and cut into 2½ cm (1 in) pieces

yakitori sauce (see following recipe)

ground sansho pepper or seven-spice mixture

1 Thread prepared livers, chicken, capsicum and leeks onto skewers. You can alternate ingredients or arrange skewers with one ingredient only, as you prefer.

2 Grill over high heat or barbecue, turning skewers, until meat is just barely cooked.

3 Dip kebabs into yakitori sauce and grill again. Continue dipping kebabs into sauce and grilling, until all sides of the kebabs are well cooked.

4 Serve seasoned with seven-spice mixture or sansho pepper.

SERVES 4

❖ **COMBINATION TEPPAN-YAKI CHARCOAL GRILL (ROBATA-YAKI)**

Robata-yaki is a combination of teppan-yaki ingredients cooked over a Japanese barbecue called a hibachi or a charcoal grill. Fish (both fresh and dried), meat, chicken, vegetables and even noodles can be used. The method is almost the same as for teppan-yaki but hibachi charcoal is used.

Robata-yaki is prepared, cooked and presented in front of the guests, and the food is served using long handled paddles. Only a skilled chef can present robata-yaki beautifully from the beginning of preparation to the serving stage. The method of serving this dish is unique — the chef serves the food to his guests from a distance using the long paddles.

Skewered Chicken

YELLOWTAIL TERIYAKI (BURI TERIYAKI)

3 tablespoons vegetable oil

4 pieces yellowtail fillets

1 cup (8 fl oz/250 ml) teriyaki sauce (see p. 59)

lemon and cucumber slices, to garnish

1 Heat oil in a pan and gently add fish pieces. Cook each side for about 3 minutes, until golden. Remove fish and set aside.
2 Pour in teriyaki sauce, add fish and spoon sauce over. Heat through, remove and arrange on a plate garnished with lemon and cucumber slices.

SERVES 4

SEAFOOD WITH PINE NEEDLES (HORAKU-YAKI)

12 large prawns (shrimps), peeled and deveined

8 pieces white-fleshed fish

12 large mushrooms

pine needles, rinsed clean

200 g (6½ oz) ginkgo nuts in shells, dry roasted

Ponzu sauce (see p. 35)

1 Gently grill prawns, fish and mushrooms.
2 Arrange a bed of pine needles on the base of a serving dish. On top place seafood, mushrooms and nuts. Garnish with a few more pine needles and serve with Ponzu sauce.

SERVES 4

YAKITORI SAUCE

½ cup (4 fl oz/125 ml) soy sauce

½ cup (4 fl oz/125 ml) mirin wine

4 tablespoons sugar

Combine the ingredients in a saucepan and bring to the boil to burn off alcohol.

YIELDS 1 CUP (8 FL OZ/250 ML)

Japanese Mixed Seafood Grill (p. 62)

JAPANESE MIXED SEAFOOD GRILL (SAKANA)

Sakana consists of a selection of seasonal fish and seafood, eg garfish, jewfish cutlets, barramundi, salmon cutlets and snapper cutlets. Rainbow trout may be used for this dish but it must be wrapped in foil as the flesh is extremely delicate and may fall apart on heating. This method is similar to steam cooking. It retains the shape of the fish and makes the removal of bones easier.

1 green lobster

5 green prawns (shrimps)

1 blue swimmer crab

5 yabbies

6 scallops or oysters

oil for brushing

salt and pepper

2 onions

5 Japanese mushrooms, soaked in warm water for 5 minutes

2 tomatoes, thickly sliced

2 capsicums (peppers), cut into thick rings

2 spring onion stalks, cut into 7½ cm (3 in) lengths

2 bamboo shoots, cut into 5 cm (2 in) lengths

TO SERVE

soy bean, sesame, and sweet mustard pastes

horseradish

soy sauce with garlic

1 Brush the raw seafood with oil, season with salt and pepper and set aside for 10 minutes.

2 Slice the onion thickly, securing each slice with a toothpick.

3 Cook the seafood on an iron barbecue at a high temperature for 5 minutes. Arrange the sliced vegetables on the grill with the seafood and cook for a further 10 minutes.

4 Serve with soy bean paste, sesame paste, sweet mustard paste, horseradish and soy sauce with garlic.

SERVES 3

JAPANESE MIXED GRILL (NIKU)

As a variation, the niku ingredients may be marinated in soy bean paste and saké for 2 to 3 hours before cooking. Other vegetables may be substituted for those in the recipe.

500 g (1 lb) eye fillet of beef or scotch fillet

2 onions

5 Japanese mushrooms

2 tomatoes

2 capsicums (peppers)

2 spring onion stalks

2 bamboo shoots

soy bean, sesame and sweet mustard pastes, to serve

horseradish, to serve

soy sauce with garlic, to serve

1 Cut the steak into 2½ cm (1 in) thick slices. Make a shallow criss-cross incision on one side of each piece of steak. Rub with oil, season with salt and pepper and leave for 10 minutes.

2 Cook the meat over high heat for 2 minutes, then arrange vegetables on the grill and cook for 10 minutes longer.

3 Serve niku hot with soy bean paste, sesame paste, sweet mustard paste, horseradish, and soy and garlic sauce.

SERVES 2 TO 3

DENGAKU RED AND WHITE MISO

Dengaku refers to miso-topped grilled food. Both these delicious toppings are suitable for dengaku dishes.

RED MISO

200 g (6½ oz) red miso

3 tablespoons sugar

5 tablespoons mirin wine

3 tablespoons saké

WHITE MISO

300 g (10 oz) white miso

3 tablespoons mirin wine

3 tablespoons saké

SEASONINGS

grated lemon or yuzu rind

sesame seeds

kinome leaves

1 To make red miso, combine all red miso ingredients in a pan. Bring to the boil and simmer for 2 to 3 minutes, until thickened. Follow the same procedure to make white miso, using the white miso ingredients.

2 Cool to room temperature and serve.

SCALLOPS WITH MISO (KAIBASHIRA DENGAKU)

700 g (1 lb 6 oz) scallops, cleaned, rinsed and dried

vegetable oil

dengaku red and white miso (see previous recipe)

ground toasted sesame seeds, to serve

1 Preheat oven to 200°C (400°F).

2 Place prepared scallops in an oiled baking dish. Spread red and white miso over scallops and bake for only 3 to 4 minutes in preheated oven.

3 Serve sprinkled with ground sesame seeds.

SERVES 4

EGGPLANTS WITH MISO (NASU DENGAKU)

2 medium-sized eggplants (aubergines), cut into 1 cm (½ in) slices

vegetable oil

dengaku red and white miso (see recipe above)

fresh coriander, to garnish

1 Thread eggplant onto 2 bamboo skewers, inserted through the sides of each slice to keep eggplant flat. Brush with vegetable oil and grill, turning until golden.

2 Serve spread with miso toppings and garnished with fresh coriander.

SERVES 4

STOCKS
AND
SOUPS

Every Japanese meal includes at least one soup (shirumono), usually served in a covered, lacquered bowl. The shallow, Western soup dish is not recommended; the subtle flavours and aromas of Japanese soups can be lost if the bowl is not covered.

Clear soup (suimono) can be served as a first course, halfway through the meal to refresh the palate, or right at the end. For balance and flavour, other ingredients are added to the well-flavoured stock, including fish, chicken, egg, shellfish, sliced vegetables or bean curd (tofu).

Traditional Japanese thick soups or shirumono are very much a meal in themselves. They are made from stock and miso paste, with plenty of hearty ingredients like poultry or meat.

Dashi with Vegetable Garnish, Golden Mushroom Soy Soup, Tofu Miso Soup

❖ BASIC STOCK (DASHI)

Just as a basic meat or fish stock is essential to the success of many Western dishes, so the Japanese dashi is vital to Japanese cuisine.

Like Western chefs who have found instant stock cubes convenient, Japanese cooks have also turned to packaged 'instant' dashi which dissolves in hot water. However, while many of these preparations are excellent, nothing compares to freshly-made dashi.

Classic dashi is made from konbu (dried kelp) which is simply wiped and soaked in cold water for 24 hours. Another popular form of dashi uses flaked dried bonito, a fish of the tuna family. After being dried in the open air, the bonito fillets are sold in the form of brownish sticks of 'wood'. Wrapped in plastic, they keep well in the refrigerator but are best when freshly prepared. Shave off bonito flakes with a very sharp knife or a grater just before using.

PRIMARY DASHI (ICHIBAN DASHI)

2 x 10 cm (4 in) pieces giant kelp
3 cups (24 fl oz/750 ml) cold water
25 g (1 oz) dried bonito flakes

1 Wipe kelp with a damp cloth and score flesh with a sharp knife to release the flavour. Add kelp and cold water to a pan. Heat on high, removing kelp just before the water reaches boiling point.

2 Add bonito flakes. Bring water back to the boil and simmer 2 to 3 minutes.

3 Remove pan from heat and strain dashi through muslin. Reserve kelp and bonito flakes for secondary dashi (see below).

YIELDS 6 CUPS (48 FL OZ/1½ LITRES)

SECONDARY DASHI (NIBAN DASHI)

4 cups (32 fl oz/1 litre) cold water
bonito flakes and giant kelp reserved from primary dashi
10 g (½ oz) dried bonito flakes

1 In a pan, combine water and reserved bonito flakes and kelp. Heat on high, removing kelp just before the water reaches boiling point. Add dried bonito flakes and simmer on very low for 5 minutes.

2 Strain liquid through muslin and set aside the kelp and flakes to use again in a secondary dashi.

YIELDS 6 CUPS (48 FL OZ/1½ LITRES)

SARDINE STOCK (NIBOSHI DASHI)

3 cups (24 fl oz/750 ml) water or dashi
30 g (1 oz) dried sardines

1 Combine ingredients in a pan and bring to the boil. Lower heat and simmer for 3 to 5 minutes.

2 Strain and use as a base for udon noodle dishes and in strong, thick miso soups.

YIELDS 6 CUPS (48 FL OZ/1½ LITRES)

VEGETABLE BROTH (SANSAI)

Sansai is a combination of various vegetables served in clear stock. It is a very simple dish to prepare and has a distinctive flavour.

3 cups (24 fl oz/750 ml) clear stock
selection of vegetables (such as ginkgo nuts, bracken, bamboo shoots and mushrooms)

Arrange vegetables in 5 soup bowls and pour hot stock over them.

SERVES 5

Vegetable Broth and Clear Soup with Snapper Fins

1 sa

2 cu

3 th
o

a
l
l
c
l

CLEAR SOUP WITH SNAPPER (USHIO JIRU)

5 small snapper fins

salt

3¾ cups (30 fl oz/900 ml) dashi

1 tablespoon soy sauce

yuzu essence (if available) or 1 cm (½ in) piece green ginger root, grated

1 spring onion stalk, finely chopped

1 Sprinkle the fins with salt and allow to stand for 15 minutes.

2 Place fins on a plate and pour boiling water over them. Allow to stand in the hot water for 15 minutes.

3 Combine dashi with the soy sauce and bring to the boil.

4 Place the fins into 5 bowls and pour the hot stock over them. Place a few drops of yuzu essence or a little grated ginger in each bowl and sprinkle with chopped spring onions.

SERVES 6 TO 8

❖ *Ushio jiru can also be made using the flesh of the fish, filleted and treated the same way as the fins. Some accompaniments or garnishes for filleted fish soup are seaweed knots, prawns and ginkgo nuts.*

STOCKS AND SOUPS 67

STEAMED FOOD
AND EGG DISHES

MUSHI-MONO AND TAMAGO-YAKI

Steaming preserves more flavour and nutrients than simmering and is particularly good for cooking very fresh food. The steamer should be very hot and steaming vigorously before food is placed in it and it is important to cook food as little as possible to gain maximum benefit.

Eggs are used in a number of different ways in Japanese cuisine, such as raw as a dipping sauce with one-pot dishes and steamed as savoury custards in small cups. Thick and thin omelettes are widely used as garnishes, as bases for sushi and rolled into decorative shapes to serve with vegetables.

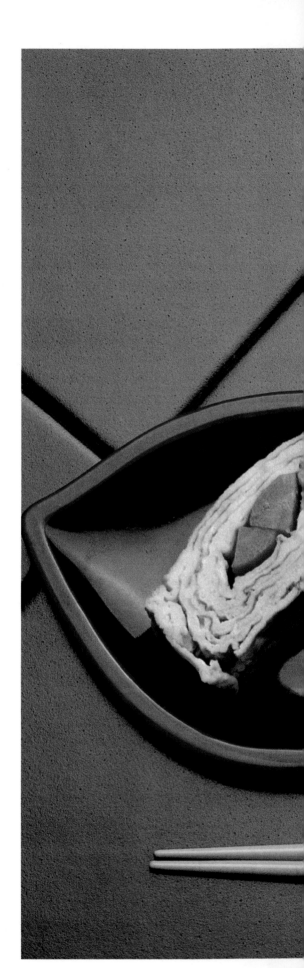

Thick omelette

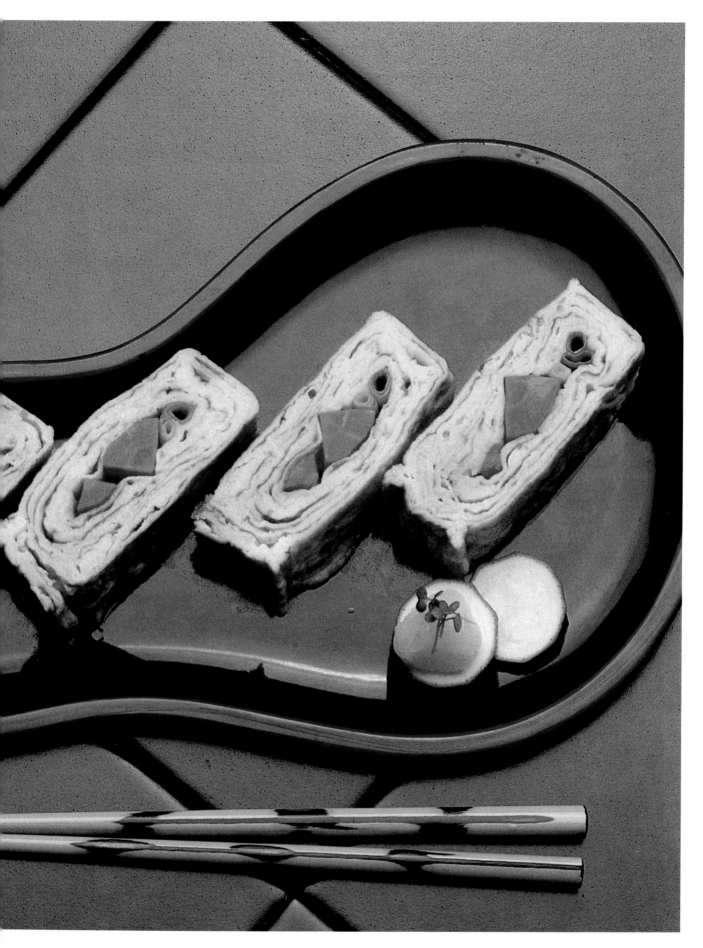

STEP-BY-STEP TECHNIQUES

1 *Beat eggs with sugar, salt and mirin.*

2 *Pour in ⅓ of mixture to cover base of omelette pan.*

3 *Place carrot and spring onion in centre.*

4 *Roll across to one side of pan.*

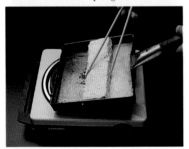

5 *Roll new mixture over cooked omelette.*

6 *Pour in final ⅓ of mixture and repeat*

THICK OMELETTE (TAMAGO-YAKI)

Japanese omelettes require a special rectangular omelette pan which makes it much easier to cook omelettes properly.

8 eggs

½ tablespoon sugar

½ tablespoon mirin wine

pinch salt

1 carrot, cooked

1 spring onion, cooked

oil

½ cup grated daikon, to serve

1 tablespoon soy sauce, to serve

1 Beat eggs with sugar, mirin and salt.

2 Heat omelette pan with a little oil until very hot. Gently pour in a third of mixture to cover base of omelette pan. Place carrot and spring onion in centre of omelette and roll across to other side of pan.

3 Pour a little oil into empty section of pan and pour in another third of mixture. Lift cooked omelette and let mixture slide underneath. From opposite side of pan, roll new mixture over cooked omelette, making a square double omelette.

4 Move to back of pan and repeat with final third of mixture making a square triple omelette.

5 Cut omelette into 2½ cm (1 in) strips and serve with grated daikon and soy sauce.

SERVES 4

FISH CAKES (NERIMONO)

500 g (1 lb) fillet of snapper, cod or barramundi

1 carrot, sliced into 10 cm (4 in) lengths

1 thick spring onion stalk

MARINADE

2 tablespoons mirin wine

pinch salt

1 tablespoon cornflour

TO SERVE

wasabi

soy sauce

basil seeds

mustard cress

1 Skin and bone the fillets of fish. Chop or mash them finely.

2 TO PREPARE MARINADE: Combine ingredients and pour over the fish. Marinate for 3 minutes.

3 Spread fish mixture over a sheet of kitchen paper and form into a 12½ cm (5 in) square approximately 2½ cm (1 in) thick.

4 Blanch the carrot sticks in boiling salted water for 2 minutes and drain. Place the carrot and spring onion onto the centre of the fish mixture.

5 Using the kitchen paper, roll the fish mixture tightly over the vegetables and twist the ends to form a bon-bon. Place the bon-bon into a steamer and steam for 20 minutes. Remove from heat and unwrap.

6 Cut into 2½ cm (1 in) pieces and serve with wasabi, soy sauce, basil seeds and mustard cress.

SERVES 2 TO 3

Fish Cakes

THIN OMELETTE (USUYAKI TAMAGO)

3 eggs

3 teaspoons sugar

pinch salt

oil, for frying

1 Combine omelette ingredients lightly with a fork, then strain mixture into a bowl.

2 Heat the omelette pan with a little oil until very hot.

3 Pour in a small quantity of egg mixture, tilting pan to spread egg out thinly.

4 Cook for a few minutes until omelette is solid, then flip over and cook other side for a few seconds. Remove and set aside to cool.

5 Repeat with remaining egg mixture. Use as required.

MAKES 4 OMELETTES

Steamed Abalone

STEAMED ABALONE (SAKA-MUSHI)

2 fresh abalone in the shell

3 tablespoons salt

½ cup (4 fl oz/125 ml) saké

dried seaweed, to garnish

SAUCE

2 tablespoons dashi

2 teaspoons soy sauce

1 teaspoon grated lemon rind

1 Rub salt well into the abalone meat, then rinse off salt and grit under a running tap.

2 Cut abalone from shell and trim edges. Place in a pan with saké, cover and cook in a steamer for 15 to 20 minutes until tender.

3 Allow to cool, then cut abalone diagonally into 1 cm (½ in) pieces. Arrange back in shells. Garnish with seaweed and serve with sauce.

4 TO MAKE SAUCE: Simply combine sauce ingredients in a small bowl.

SERVES 4

SAKÉ STEAMED CHICKEN (TORINIKU SHIO-MUSHI)

750 g (1 lb 8 oz) Chicken Maryland pieces (thigh and drumstick)

salt

3 tablespoons fresh lemon juice

½ cup (4 fl oz/125 ml) saké

2 teaspoons grated ginger

SAUCE

3 tablespoons soy sauce

1 teaspoon grated ginger

1 Pierce chicken skin and place chicken pieces in a small dish. Sprinkle with salt, lemon juices, saké and grated ginger.

2 Place dish inside a steamer. Cover and cook for about 20 minutes on high.

3 Take chicken from dish, remove bones and cut chicken into small pieces. Arrange on a serving platter.

4 Serve hot or cold.

5 **TO PREPARE SAUCE:** Ingredients should be combined and either served separately as a dipping sauce, or poured over the chicken pieces.

SERVES 6

SAVOURY EGG CUSTARD (CHAWAN-MUSHI)

200 g (7 oz) chicken fillets, cut into bite-sized pieces

2 teaspoons saké

2 teaspoons soy sauce

2 leeks, sliced

½ carrot, sliced

½ bunch spinach, chopped

CUSTARD

4 cups (32 fl oz/1 litre) dashi

2 tablespoons soy sauce

6 eggs

1 Place the chicken pieces into 6 heatproof bowls. Combine saké and soy sauce, and pour over chicken.

2 Divide vegetables between the 6 bowls.

3 **TO PREPARE CUSTARD:** Combine custard ingredients and strain equal amounts into the bowls.

4 Cover with foil and place in a steamer. Cook on high for 20 to 30 minutes. Test by inserting a fine skewer in the centre. The custard is cooked when the skewer has no moisture clinging to it.

SERVES 6

Savoury egg custard, served here with prawns, lily root and zucchini (courgette)

MAKUNOUCHI
DINNER BOXES

A traditional makunouchi lunch or dinner box contains no less than 8 or 10 different foods. Rice moulds, grilled fish, sashimi, pickles, sweets, prawns and vegetables are all suitable. Try a selection of the following: cooked Japanese mushrooms, oyster mushrooms, dressed-up prawns (shrimps), pickles, grilled sayori (garfish), rolled omelettes, marrons glacés, yaki-tofu (grilled tofu), fish cakes, calamari sashimi, rolled beef and makunouchi rice (boiled, white glutinous rice formed into a cylindrical shape in special moulds, cut into 3 cm [1½ in] lengths and sprinkled with sesame seeds).

The ingredients are presented in decorative lacquer boxes in combinations carefully arranged for artistic effect. Many years ago in Japan, people used to pack a makunouchi lunch and take it with them to eat while watching Sumo wrestling. These days lunch boxes can be bought at railway stations in the Japanese countryside, each area having its own specialities.

Makunouchi Dinner Box

PICKLES

Traditionally, the most basic Japanese meal consists of rice and pickles. Such frugality is rarely found these days although some old people still consider this combination to be an adequate repast. In Buddhist monasteries, where asceticism is a way of life, rice, pickles and a few vegetables are all that sustain life.

Pickles are much more to the Japanese than a condiment — they are a staple food of great importance. Once every Japanese family boasted a large pickle barrel from which the household supplies were taken daily. Commercially produced pickles are more usual today. Pickles are relished for their piquant flavours, their sharp, cleansing effect on the palate and as an aid to digestion. Although many of them seem overpowering at first to the uninitiated westerner, a taste for their unique flavours and aromas, which complement a Japanese meal so well, is soon acquired.

Pickled Radish and Eggplant Pickles

HILLY ROOT VEGETABLES (YAMA-GOBOU)

This pickling method for hilly root vegetables is called shoyu-zuke — pickling of vegetables with soy sauce.

5 yama-gobou (see Glossary)
1 cup (8 fl oz/250 ml) soy sauce
1 tablespoon mirin wine
50 g (2 oz) chopped basil

1 Wash, scrape and dry the yama-gobou.
2 Combine the soy with the mirin and basil in a bowl.
3 Place the vegetables into this pickling solution and marinate for one week.
4 After 1 week, cut the vegetables into 7½ cm (3 in) lengths and serve.

EGGPLANT (NASU)

5 x 7½ cm (3 in) long baby eggplants (aubergines)
¼ cup (2 oz/60 g) salt

MARINADE
200 g (6½ oz) miso paste
2 tablespoons mirin wine
2 tablespoons grated ginger

1 Wash and dry eggplants and rub with the salt. Place eggplants onto a wire rack and allow moisture to escape from the skin.
2 TO PREPARE MARINADE: Combine the miso paste, mirin and grated ginger in a bowl. Place the salted eggplants into the bottom of a plastic container and pour the marinade over.
3 Cover the container and allow the eggplants to pickle for 1 week before using.
4 Serve whole or halved as an accompaniment to any meal.

PLUM PICKLES (UMEBOSHI)

The Japanese call this type of pickling 'young pickles' because they are only marinated for 1 week. If more mature pickles are desired, the marinating period is extended to 1 month but extra salt and another 2 tablespoons of sugar must be added during the pickling process to prevent bacterial growth. If care is taken during preparation, the plum pickles may be kept for up to 6 months. During this time the plums shrivel and the flavour develops a great deal. The Japanese believe that pickled plums aid the digestion of food and provide fibre in the diet.

24 small unblemished plums
2 cups (16 oz/500 g) salt
2 cups (16 fl oz/500 ml) saké
5 violet-coloured basil leaves
2 drops red food colouring

1 Scrub each plum with ¼ cup (2 oz/60 g) of the salt and soak overnight in cold water. Remove from water and drain.
2 Combine saké with remaining 1¾ cups (12 oz/380 g) salt and place in a large container. Add basil leaves and food colouring and mix.
3 Add the plums. Seal the container and place a heavy weight on the lid.
4 Store in a cool place for 1 week, stirring once during that time.

CABBAGE IN VINEGAR PICKLES (KYABETSU SU-ZUKE)

½ cabbage
¾ cup (6 oz/185 g) sugar
4 tablespoons salt
8 cups (64 fl oz/2 litres) rice vinegar

1 Remove core from cabbage, wash and cut into small wedges. Pack pieces into preserving jar.

2 Make a syrup of the sugar, salt and vinegar by bringing quickly to the boil. Stir to dissolve the sugar.

3 Pour syrup over cabbage and cover.

4 Can be served after 3 days, and will keep for up to 6 weeks.

SALTED TURNIP PICKLES (KABU NO SOKUSEKI-ZUKE)

18 turnips, peeled and cut into very thin strips

3 tablespoons salt

1 teaspoon grated lemon rind

1 Rub turnip strips gently with salt. Place in a bowl with lemon rind, and cover.

2 May be served in 2 hours, or left for a few days to absorb more salt.

3 Serve in very small quantities.

RICE BRAN PICKLED CABBAGE (KYABETSU NO NUKA-ZUKE)

½ cabbage, washed and cut into thin slices

800 g (1 lb 8 oz) rock salt

800 g (1 lb 8 oz) rice bran

3 small dried red chillies, seeded and finely chopped

3 teaspoons grated ginger

1 Using a large earthenware pot or dish, make layers of cabbage slices, salt and rice bran. Sprinkle chillies and ginger throughout.

2 Cover and leave for at least 4 weeks. Use as required.

PICKLED RADISH (TAKU-AN)

A selection of Japanese pickles

This method of pickling is called nuka-zuke. During the summertime taku-an may need to stand for only 3 days for flavours to develop. Once the seal is broken it must be refrigerated to prevent spoilage but will keep for up to 3 months.

Taku-an is eaten as an afternoon snack or with the main meal or rice dishes. If daikon is unavailable turnip may be used instead.

1 daikon

½ cup (4 oz/125 g) salt

3½ cups (1 lb/500 g) rice bran

2 cups (16 fl oz/500 ml) water

1 tablespoon turmeric

3 whole dried chillies

soy sauce, to serve

1 Cut stalks off end of daikon and rub the entire vegetable with salt.

2 Combine the rice bran with water, turmeric and chillies and mix well.

3 Add whole daikon to the mixture and place into a plastic container. Seal, place a brick on top of lid and allow to stand for 1 week before using in order to give flavours time to develop.

4 Serve sliced with soy sauce.

FOODS IN VINEGAR
OR DRESSING

SUNOMONO AND AEMONO

Western cuisine uses a side salad to complement the main course. The Japanese equivalent is sunomono and aemono. These are served in vinegar and dressing and combine seafood and fruit.

Aemono means 'dressed'; these dressings are usually thicker and more heavily flavoured than sunomono 'vinegary' dressings. Be careful not to add too much dressing to the recipe or you will spoil the flavour. Another important factor is to ensure that the ingredients are cold and well dried before adding the dressing.

Golden Mushrooms and Seaweed

GOLDEN MUSHROOMS (MIZOREAE)

Mizoreae does not require any cooking and is served cold. It makes a refreshing breakfast or it can be served at lunch or dinner accompanied by steaming rice. The rice is good with soy sauce and raw egg stirred through it before serving.

200 g (6½ oz) golden mushrooms (nameko)

100 g (3 oz) grated daikon

3 tablespoons soy sauce

1 sheet dried seaweed, to garnish

1 Combine the mushrooms and grated daikon gently with the soy sauce.

2 Arrange on a serving plate and garnish with thinly sliced seaweed.

SERVES 2

CRAB (KANI-NO-SUNOMONO)

Mud crabs may be substituted for blue swimmer crabs in this dish. In Japan, the Japanese snow crab called taraba-gani is used.

2 large blue swimmer crabs, uncooked

1 tablespoon salt

3 pieces lotus root, to garnish

MARINADE

1 cup (8 fl oz/250 ml) vinegar

¼ cup (2 oz/60 g) sugar

1 small piece kelp

¾ cup (6 fl oz/180 ml) water

1 Place the crabs in a large saucepan of cold water with the salt and bring to the boil. Turn crabs over and cook on high heat for 20 minutes. Remove from hot water and plunge into icy cold water. Remove and drain.

2 Clean the crabs by removing the guts. Separate the crab legs from the body.

3 TO PREPARE MARINADE: Mix together vinegar, sugar, kelp and water. Add the crab and marinate for 30 minutes.

4 Place the lotus root in a bowl of warm water and soak until it swells up.

5 Remove crab from marinade and arrange on a plate to resemble whole crabs. Garnish with the lotus root and serve.

SERVES 2

WHITING (KISU-NO-SUNOMONO)

The technique of combining kelp with the whiting flesh is called kobu-jime.

2 King George whiting

1 sheet dried kelp

3 tablespoons salt

MARINADE

¼ cup (2 fl oz/60 ml) mirin wine

1 cup (8 fl oz/250 ml) white vinegar

1 cup (8 fl oz/250 ml) water

cucumber flower, or cucumber peel spirals, to garnish

1 Clean and scale the whiting. Fillet, removing all bones.

2 Soak the dried kelp in warm water for 15 minutes. Remove kelp and cut into 4 equal pieces.

3 Place each fillet onto a piece of the kelp and press so it adheres. Sprinkle the salt over the fish fillets and allow to stand for 15 minutes.

4 TO PREPARE MARINADE: Combine the mirin and vinegar with a cup of water and pour over the whiting fillets. Allow to marinate for 1 hour.

5 Remove the fillets from the marinade and slice thinly, sashimi style. Arrange slices on a plate, kelp side down, and garnish with a cucumber flower or cucumber peel spiral.

SERVES 2

Crab

OCTOPUS (TAKO)

Octopus is another type of seafood which the Japanese eat frequently. Octopus prepared in a food press and roasted (called tako-yaki) is a much prized Japanese delicacy.

1 medium-sized octopus
ice-cold water
wasabi or soy sauce, to serve

MARINADE
1 small cucumber
1 cup (8 fl oz/250 ml) vinegar
¼ cup (2 oz/60 g) sugar
1 small piece dried kelp

1 Wash octopus and cook as for tako recipe in sashimi section (p. 29). Plunge octopus into icy water to cool and drain.
2 Remove seeds from cucumber and slice into thin strips with the skin on.
3 TO PREPARE MARINADE: Combine cucumber with vinegar, sugar and kelp and use to marinate the octopus for 1 hour.
4 Remove octopus from marinade and thinly slice into 2½ cm (1 in) pieces. Arrange on a plate and serve with wasabi or soy sauce.

SERVES 2 TO 3

MARINATED GARFISH (SAYORI NO-SUZUKE)

Marinating foods in a sweet and sour sauce is called suzuke. Marinated garfish can be used for nigiri-zushi and sashimi as well.

4 medium-sized fresh garfish
2 tablespoons salt
1 small piece dried kelp, cut into 8 strips
wasabi, to serve
soy sauce, to serve

MARINADE
1 cup (8 fl oz/250 ml) white vinegar
¼ cup (2 oz/60 g) sugar

1 Clean and fillet the garfish, discarding the head, tail, fins and bones. Sprinkle salt over the fillets on the skin side and allow to stand for 15 minutes.
2 Attach 1 strip of kelp to the underside of each fillet.
3 TO PREPARE MARINADE: Mix vinegar and sugar together. Arrange each fillet (kelp side down) in a flat, shallow dish, pour the marinade over and allow to stand for 30 minutes.
4 Carefully lift out each fillet and serve on a plate accompanied by wasabi and soy sauce.

SERVES 4

JELLYFISH (KURAGE)

Jellyfish is readily available in Japan but in other countries it is more difficult to obtain. Although the thought of eating jellyfish is distasteful to many westerners, it does have a distinct and quite acceptable texture and flavour when prepared Japanese style — it remains soft on the outside whilst the internal texture is quite crunchy.

200 g (6½ oz) salted jellyfish
seaweed, thinly sliced, to serve
soy sauce, to serve

MARINADE
1 small cucumber, seeded and cut into long strips
1 cup (8 fl oz/250 ml) vinegar (su)
¼ cup (2 oz/60 g) sugar
1 very small piece dried kelp

1 Wash jellyfish, place into a dish of cold water and soak for 30 minutes to remove excess salt. Remove and drain.
2 TO PREPARE MARINADE: Combine cucumber strips with the vinegar, sugar and kelp in a bowl. Add jellyfish and marinate for 1 hour.
3 Remove from marinade and arrange on a small plate sprinkled with thinly sliced seaweed. Soy sauce may be served as an accompaniment.

SERVES 2

STEP-BY-STEP TECHNIQUES

SEAWEED (NUTA)

This dish goes well as a snack with saké.

200 g (6½ oz) wakame

radish rose, to garnish

MARINADE

1 tablespoon sesame seeds, toasted and ground

½ cup (4 oz/125 g) hot miso paste

1½ tablespoons mirin wine

¼ cup (2 oz/60 g) sugar

¼ cup (2 fl oz/60 ml) vinegar

2 spring onions, chopped

1 Soak wakame in warm water for 10 minutes.

2 TO PREPARE MARINADE: Mix sesame seeds with the hot miso paste, mirin, sugar, vinegar and chopped spring onions.

3 Remove seaweed from water and chop into 5 cm (2 in) pieces. Add to the marinade and allow to stand for 3 minutes.

4 Remove seaweed from marinade, arrange on a dish and garnish with a radish rose.

1 *Soak wakame in water.*

2 *Mix ground sesame seeds with miso paste, mirin, sugar and spring onions.*

3 *Add seaweed to mixture.*

DESSERTS

JAPANESE-STYLE FRUIT

In Japan fresh fruit is served as a dessert after the main meal of the day. The Japanese are very particular about the way their food looks and expect their fruit to be presented in an appealing way in order to bring their meal to a satisfying conclusion. Preparation and presentation of fruit is done with extreme care in order to preserve the beauty of each individual piece.

Sometimes fruit served for dessert is accompanied by sweet beans (azuki), sweet bean ice-cream (ogura-ice), or plum wine liqueur. The illustration on the right demonstrates one of many ways of presenting fruit Japanese-style.

SWEETS

Made in the shapes of fruit and flowers, 'tea-sweets' are served as part of the ritual of the tea ceremony. Nowadays, however, Western-style cakes and confections are beginning to replace the Japanese sweets in popularity.

A selection of Japanese fruit

SWEET RED-BEAN SOUP (ZENZAI)

200 g (6½ oz) red-beans, soaked in cold water overnight

1¼ cups (6½ oz/200 g) brown sugar

pinch salt

2 rice cakes (mochi), grilled

1 sheet dried seaweed, cut into 4

pickled plums or pickled baby eggplants (aubergines), to serve

1 Drain beans and place in a saucepan of cold water. Bring to the boil and simmer for 3 hours or until very tender.

2 Add sugar and salt and stir until well mixed and the sugar dissolved. Cook for another 30 minutes.

3 Grill the rice cakes until slightly golden.

4 Wet fingers and form each piece of seaweed into a small bundle.

5 Cut rice cakes in half. Place 1 piece of rice cake and a bundle of seaweed in each of 4 bowls and pour the hot red-bean mixture over. Serve hot on its own or with pickled prunes or pickled baby eggplants.

SERVES 4

RICE AND BEAN PASTE BALLS (OHAGI)

300 g (10 oz) mochi (sticky rice)

salt

300 g (10 oz) sweet red-bean paste

4 tablespoons roasted soybean flour (kinako)

1 Season cooked rice with salt to taste. Purée in a blender, adding sufficient water to make a thick paste.

2 Shape red-bean paste into balls and surround each with a thick layer of rice paste.

3 Roll in kinako and serve.

MAKES ABOUT 12 BALLS

SWEET RED-BEAN PASTE (KOSHI-AN)

200 g (6½ oz) azuki beans, soaked in cold water overnight

1¼ cups (8 oz/250 g) sugar

1 Place beans in a pan with 4 cups (32 fl oz/ 1 litre) water. Bring to boil and simmer until the beans are soft.

2 Remove beans with a slotted spoon to a sieve. Place the sieve over the bean water in the pan. Press beans with the back of a wooden spoon so pulp strains into the bean water.

3 Pour this mixture through a muslin cloth and wring out the liquid.

4 Place pulp in a clean pan, stir in sugar and keep stirring over low heat until paste thickens.

5 Cool and serve.

YIELDS 2 CUPS (1 LB/500 G)

INSTANT SWEETENED RED-BEAN PASTE (KOSHI-AN)

Sarashi-an is an instant red-bean paste available in powdered form.

120 g (4 oz) sarashi-an

1 cup (8 fl oz/250 ml) boiling water

1 cup (7 oz/220 g) sugar

1 Combine sarashi-an and 1 cup (8 fl oz/ 250 ml) boiling water in a bowl and set aside.

2 When the bean paste starts to solidify at the bottom of the dish, carefully skim off the water above.

3 Pour paste and water mixture into a muslin bag and wring out liquid.

4 Place remaining pulp in a pan, stir in the sugar and continue stirring over low heat until paste thickens.

5 Cool and serve.

YIELDS ABOUT 3 CUPS (1 LB 8 OZ/750 G)

JELLIED FRUIT (MITSUMAME)

5 g (⅙ oz) agar-agar strands (about 30)

1 cup (8 fl oz/250 ml) water

1 tablespoon sugar

2 mandarins, quartered

2 peaches, cut into slices

2 kiwi fruit, cut into slices

orange liqueur, to serve

SYRUP

¾ cup (6 oz/185 g) sugar

1½ cups (12 fl oz/360 ml) water

1 tablespoon orange liqueur

1 Cut agar-agar into 2½ cm (1 in) pieces. Soak in water for 1 hour. Rinse under cold running water and wring out.

2 Cook agar-agar gently in a pan with the water. Stir only when all the agar-agar has dissolved.

3 Add sugar and cook for 5 more minutes.

4 Strain mixture into a baking dish. Cover and refrigerate for about 12 hours.

5 TO PREPARE SYRUP: Combine water and sugar in a saucepan. Add liqueur and boil to dissolve sugar. Cool, then refrigerate.

6 Cut jelly into squares. Serve topped with sliced fresh fruit sprinkled with liqueur.

SERVES 4

Sweet Red-bean Soup

RICE CAKES WITH SWEET RED-BEANS (DAIFUKU)

1 cup (7 oz/220 g) red-beans (azuki), soaked in cold water overnight

½ cup (4 oz/125 g) sugar

2 tablespoons saké

pinch salt

1 cup (6 oz/185 g) mochi-gome

¼ cup (2 fl oz/60 ml) warm water

½ cup (2 oz/60 g) shinko (confectioner's flour)

flour, to dust board

1 Drain beans and replace in a saucepan of cold water. Bring to the boil and simmer for 3 hours or until tender.

2 Add sugar, saké and salt and stir until the sugar has dissolved. Cook for a further 30 minutes. Remove from heat and cool.

3 Using a mortar and pestle, grind the rice to a smooth paste. Add ¼ cup (2 fl oz/60 ml) warm water and stir in the shinko to form a soft dough.

4 Turn dough out onto a lightly floured board and knead until smooth. Roll dough out paper-thin and cut into 10 cm (4 in) squares.

5 Remove beans from the cool liquid and drain.

6 Place one soup-spoon of beans into the centre of each square and bring the corners of the dough up and over the filling. Shape into a round and twist the corners. Turn the rounds upside down so the smooth side faces upwards.

7 Arrange the daifuku on a plate and serve with Japanese green tea as an afternoon tea treat.

SERVES 4 TO 6

CHUNKY SWEET RED-BEAN PASTE (TSUBUSHI-AN)

200 g (6½ oz) azuki beans

1 cup (8 oz/250 g) sugar

1 Cook beans as for Sweet Red-bean Paste (see p. 90) but for longer, until beans are very soft.

2 Return to heat, add sugar and stir gently over a low heat. The beans will be so soft that they will begin to disintegrate during stirring.

3 The desired consistency is a thick, pulpy mixture in which the beans are only half-crushed.

YIELDS 2 CUPS (16 OZ/500 G)

ICED TEA (UJI GORI)

1¼ cups (9½ oz/300 g) sugar

3 teaspoons powdered green tea

6 cups (1 lb 5 oz/660 g) shaved ice

lemon peel, to garnish

1 Place sugar and water in a pan and bring to the boil. Stir until sugar has dissolved.

2 Simmer until the liquid thickens slightly. Cool liquid, add tea and stir.

4 Make a dome of ice shavings on each of 6 plates. Pour over the syrup, garnish with lemon peel and serve.

SERVES 6

STEP-BY-STEP TECHNIQUES

YOKAN JELLY (MIZU-YOKAN)

If substituting gelatine for agar-agar, the yokan will not have the same texture or delicacy.

5 g (⅙ oz) agar-agar strands (about 30), or gelatine

1 tablespoon sugar

350 g (11 oz) sweet red-bean paste, puréed

green yokan and candied chestnuts, to decorate

1 Soak agar-agar for 20 minutes in cold water. Rinse under running tap and wring out.

2 Break into tiny pieces. Add to saucepan with sugar and 1 cup (8 fl oz/250 ml) cold water. Cook gently without stirring until agar-agar has dissolved. Skim off foam and stir.

3 Add bean paste and boil for 5 minutes on high.

4 Pour into a bowl and cool quickly by placing the bowl in a sink filled with cold water. When mixture is thick but of pouring consistency, pour into small sweet dishes, and decorate with green yokan squares and candied chestnuts.

5 Leave jelly overnight to set.

6 Cut neatly into squares with a sharp knife ensuring that each serve contains a piece of yokan or a candied chestnut.

SERVES 6

1 Dissolve agar-agar in hot water.

2 When melted, pour into tin.

3 Using chopsticks, drop green yokan and candied chestnuts into agar-agar and allow to set.

Yokan Jelly

CANDIED CHESTNUTS (KURI-NO-AMA-NI)

375 g (12 oz) raw chestnuts, shelled
225 g (7 oz) crystallised sugar
1½ cups (12 fl oz/360 ml) water
yellow food colouring
yokan jelly or fresh fruit, to serve

1 Carve chestnuts into an angular shape. Place in a bowl of water and leave to soak for about 24 hours.

2 Bring sugar and water slowly to the boil. Simmer for 5 minutes to thicken.

3 Add food colouring and chestnuts and bring to the boil again. Lower heat and cook for a further 1 1/2 hours. Transfer to a bowl and leave for 48 hours before serving.

4 Serve chestnuts without the syrup, accompanied by Yokan jelly (see p. 93), or fresh fruit.

SERVES 6

Candied Chestnuts and Yokan Squares

STRAWBERRY JELLY (AWAYUKI)

The word awayuki means 'snow drift'.

4 cups (32 fl oz/1 litre) hot water
10 g (½ oz) agar-agar
4 egg whites
1 punnet strawberries
½ cup (4 oz/125 g) sugar
¼ cup (2 fl oz/60 ml) plum wine or Cointreau
¼ cup (2 fl oz/60 ml) milk
ice-cream or semi-whipped cream, to serve

1 Break the agar-agar into pieces and place in pan with 4 cups (32 fl oz/1 litre) of hot water. Bring to the boil and heat on low temperature for 10 minutes.

2 Add sugar and plum wine and stir until combined and the sugar dissolved. Pour the hot liquid through a strainer and reserve.

3 Beat egg whites in a bowl until stiff. Fold the egg whites and milk through the warm liquid and pour mixture into a rectangular, plastic mould.

4 Cut stems off strawberries and arrange in rows in the mixture. Place in refrigerator to set and cool.

5 When set, cut into squares and serve either on its own or with ice-cream or semi-whipped cream.

SERVES 6

INDEX

ENJOY A WORLD OF GOOD COOKING WITH THE
BAY BOOKS COOKERY COLLECTION

If these titles are not available from your regular stockists, please contact the HarperCollins Sales Office in your State:

WESTERN AUSTRALIA

SUITE 2 , 25 BELGRAVIA ST

BELMONT WA 6104

TEL: (09) 479 4988

FAX: (09) 478 3248

SOUTH AUSTRALIA

UNIT 1 , 1-7 UNION ST

STEPNEY SA 5069

TEL: (08) 363 0122

FAX: (08) 363 1653

QUEENSLAND

643 KESSELS ROAD

UPPER MOUNT GRAVATT

QLD 4122

TEL: (07) 849 7855

FAX: (07) 349 8286

VICTORIA

22-24 JOSEPH STREET

NORTH BLACKBURN

VIC 3130

TEL: (03) 895 8100

FAX: (03) 895 8199

NEW SOUTH WALES

25 RYDE ROAD

PYMBLE NSW 2073

TEL: (02) 952 5000

FAX: (02) 952 5777